AIR ATLANTIQUE

CHARLES WOODLEY

AMBERLEY

First published 2021

Amberley Publishing
The Hill, Stroud,
Gloucestershire, GL5 4EP

www.amberley-books.com

ISBN: 978 1 4456 9316 3 (print)
ISBN: 978 1 4456 9317 0 (ebook)

British Library Cataloguing in Publication Data.
A catalogue record for this book is available from the British Library.

Typeset in 10pt on 13pt Celeste.
Origination by Amberley Publishing.
Printed in the UK.

Contents

Introduction   4

1   The Early Days   5

2   Diversification   8

3   Showtime   50

4   The Rundown   78

    Appendix 1   89

    Appendix 2   91

    Appendix 3   93

    Acknowledgements   95

Introduction

This is the story of a unique airline. A British airline. The brainchild of a proud Yorkshireman who managed it throughout its unusual life and gave a new working life to a collection of ageing airliners that had been pensioned off by the major world airlines. An airline that was to diversify into maritime pollution control and surveillance, mail and newspaper contract haulage, scheduled passenger operations, aircraft overhauls, air displays and pleasure flying, and the management of its own airport. A group of companies that would be beset by circumstances that resulted in the termination of passenger charter work, the hiving off of many subsidiaries through management buyouts, and the closure of its main airport base by an unsympathetic new owner. The refusal of its founder to see the random disposal of the large collection of historic aircraft he had built up over the years, and the consequent establishment of a new aircraft museum to preserve them and display them to the public. This is the story of the Air Atlantique group of companies, and a man with a vision and a love of old aeroplanes.

As an aviation enthusiast, I had followed the fortunes of the airline since its inception, toured its base at Coventry on several occasions, attended its unrivalled air shows there, and enjoyed pleasure flights in several of its aircraft. After the airline ceased to function I searched for books covering its history and, apart from an excellent volume on the aircraft of the Classic Flight produced by one of its luminaries, I failed to find one. Thus, this book came about. Appeals for assistance brought forth reminiscences, photos and offers of help from a gratifying number of former staff members, and thanks to them I can claim that much of the material in this book is appearing for the first time. It is obvious that the airline is fondly remembered by those who kept it running, and one of my regrets is that I never worked for Air Atlantique. This book is dedicated to all those who did, and especially to its founder, Mike Collett.

1

The Early Days

Michael John Hirst Collett was born in 1943 in Doncaster, Yorkshire. While at school he enrolled in that establishment's Combined Cadet Force and, having been bitten by the aviation bug, chose to join the RAF section, as this would offer him the opportunity to undergo pilot training and qualify for a Private Pilot's Licence. From school he went on to Leeds University to study textiles but left after two years, having been smitten by a desire to try and earn a living from flying. Uncertain as to how to accomplish this, he wrote to several airlines for advice and an application form. One of them, the leading independent carrier British United Airways (BUA), was sponsoring promising pilot applicants through the training course for a Commercial Pilot's Licence. His application was successful, and BUA sent him off to Air Service Training at Perth in Scotland to study for his Instrument Rating. He gained his Commercial Pilot's Licence in 1968, but by then the airline industry was in the midst of a slump. BUA had no immediate vacancy to offer him and suggested he look elsewhere in the meantime. Unsuccessful interviews followed, including one with Hunting Surveys at Elstree aerodrome, before he found employment with Westair at Blackpool Airport, flying joy-riders around the famous tower in a small Cessna 172 aircraft. Westair also used their aircraft for air taxi work, and one day he was asked to stand in for a sick pilot on one of these trips. This he successfully completed, and this type of activity gradually replaced the pleasure flying as his main work with Westair. In 1969 he accepted a position as personal pilot to a wealthy businessman with a twin-engined Cessna 401 aircraft he kept at Jersey Airport. The flying was sporadic and left him with time on his hands to consider new possibilities. With a friend he set up the company that would eventually evolve into a fully fledged airline named Air Atlantique. In the beginning, however, the pair entered the lucrative field of importing light aircraft into Britain. Flying-club-type aircraft were purchased in France, refurbished and sold on to flying schools and private owners in the UK who needed to replace their elderly fleets. This activity was carried out under the trading name of General Aviation Sales Ltd, with General Aviation Services as the parent company. The first aircraft imported were a Tiger Moth and a Stampe biplane, acquired from a Dinan-based club for £950 the pair, and shortly afterwards the company was successful in gaining the UK dealership for the modern American Aviation AA-1 and AA-5 touring aircraft. Further expansion came in 1971 with the award of an Air Operator's

Certificate, permitting the operation of air taxi services. Twin-engined Cessna 310 and 336 aircraft were acquired for this purpose and based at Jersey. A new name for this activity was thought desirable and several possibilities were looked at. In those pre-internet days, the *Yellow Pages* classified telephone directory was widely used to search for businesses offering various goods and services. The names were listed in alphabetical order, and General Aviation Services came quite a way down the list. In order to appear first in the listing, thought was given to renaming the company Aardvark Aviation, but eventually the more businesslike Air Atlantique was settled on – this name was thought of as having more appeal to Jersey's mostly French-speaking population.

By 1974 General Aviation Services had taken up an option to acquire the lease on Doncaster Airport, but it was thought that the organisation had grown too large and too geographically spread out, with around sixteen employees stationed on the UK mainland and another eight based on Jersey, and its activities needed to be split between separate companies. Mike Collett had become disenchanted with the aircraft sales side, with its assurances from buyers that 'the cheque was in the post', and from sellers that their aircraft's paperwork was all in order, when in fact neither assurance was true. It was decided that his partner would take responsibility for the aircraft sales and distribution side and the Doncaster base, leaving him to concentrate on Jersey-based air taxi services. A growing number of freight charters were being operated to northern France by then, and larger aircraft needed to be acquired if the demand was to be satisfied. When West Country Aviation put Douglas Dakota G-AMCA on the market it was purchased by Air Atlantique for £72,000. The Dakota was a short-haul twin-engined tailwheel transport aircraft, powered by Pratt & Whitney Twin Wasp radial piston engines. It had been designed to fit the requirements of the US internal airlines, and first flew in December 1935 as the DST Sleeper Transport. During the Second World War over 10,000 examples of the military C-47 version were produced, and after the war converted surplus examples flooded the airline market. Once acquired, however, G-AMCA needed to be adapted to suit Air Atlantique's requirements, and this conversion could only proceed at a slow pace. Charter enquiries were still flowing in, so when another Dakota became available for only £45,000 it was snapped up. It had previously been used by Fairey Surveys, who had installed camera hatches in its fuselage. These were still in place and would prove to be a bonus in years to come. In March 1977 Air Atlantique was registered as an operator of cargo charter flights to Europe, North Africa and the Middle East. The major (50 per cent) shareholder was General Aviation Services, the Chairman and Managing Director was MJH Collett, and the Chief Pilot was W. J. Foden. Operations officially commenced in June 1977, with the first Dakota-operated charter transporting a consignment of lobsters from Jersey to Morlaix in northern France on 19 July that year.

October 1977 proved to be a significant point in the history of Air Atlantique. During that month the airline began transporting car components between Coventry and Cologne on a regular basis, and in November of that year there was the announcement that the company would be stationing a Dakota at Coventry – the first freighter aircraft to be based at the airport for some four years. Its primary role would be the transportation of Ford car components to Continental Europe, while the airline's other Dakota was also hard at work on oil-related charter flights out of Aberdeen. It was hoped that as more automotive contracts were acquired a second Dakota could also be based at Coventry. Despite continual scare stories about the possible closure of Coventry Airport, both the airline and the airport's General Manager, Rod Rufus, said they remained confident about its long-term future. By 1978 Air Atlantique had expanded to include three Dakota aircraft and twelve employees, including Paul Sabin, who had been taken on in 1977 as operations assistant/aircraft cleaner and was to work his way up to flight deck crew member and eventually Chief Pilot before eventually leaving in 1997 to fly corporate jets. In March 1979 Air Atlantique signed up to use Coventry as its primary base for freight services throughout the UK and mainland Europe. If all went as planned this contract could be worth more than £100,000 per annum to the airport if the airline went ahead with adding two four-engined Douglas DC-6 freighters to the Dakotas already based there. This would boost the cargo throughput to 1,500 tons each year – the highest since 1973. In fact, the only problem the airport manager could foresee was that the national fuel shortage affecting the country at that period might delay this expansion, as Air Atlantique's fuel uptake requirement would be doubling and this might be difficult to meet. In May of that year two long-range DC-6B aircraft acquired from Greenlandair arrived in the UK. The DC-6B was the passenger variant of the Douglas DC-6, which was itself a pressurised development of the DC-4 transport. It was powered by four Pratt & Whitney Double Wasp piston engines and had originally been widely used on transatlantic services by the major airlines. However, the knock-on effects of the oil crisis of the late 1970s meant that these aircraft, appropriately re-registered G-SIXA and G-SIXB, were no longer viable and they would leave Air Atlantique by the end of the year. G-SIXA went straight into storage at Manston Airport in Kent as a source of spare parts, eventually being broken up there. G-SIXB was despatched to Africa to operate flights for Air Cargo Swaziland before being sold in the USA.

Dakota G-AMRA landing at Jersey – still in the basic livery of its previous operator, Eastern Airways. (Courtesy of Rosemary Ames)

2

Diversification

Air Atlantique became involved with another aircraft type at the beginning of the 1980s. The air charter broker Instone Air Line had purchased a twin-engined Bristol 170 freighter from the Royal New Zealand Air Force for cargo and livestock haulage, and after arrival in the UK in March 1981 and overhaul it was based at Stansted Airport. From there Air Atlantique operated it on behalf of Instone, wearing hybrid Instone/ Atlantic titles and later in their own livery. The type's capacious freight hold and large nose-doors enabled it to accommodate unusual consignments and it was kept busy flying racehorses into Stansted for onward transportation to the stables at Newmarket, and on scheduled freight services from Lydd to Beauvais and Rotterdam. It also carried out varied ad hoc charter flights, transporting electronic equipment from Coventry to Reyjakvik in Iceland, Airbus A320 main landing gear assemblies from Staverton to Toulouse, and even a polar expedition complete with its husky dogs and tents from Oslo to Heathrow. A second Bristol 170, ZK-EPD, was later imported from New Zealand, arriving in the UK in September 1982. This machine was later sold in Canada and by the beginning of 1987 the company's sole example, G-BISU, was the last one still flying commercially in the world. After retirement by Air Atlantique it too went to an operator in Canada.

In the meantime, the Dakotas were found more new assignments. In July 1980 Air Atlantique teamed up with Pionair Tours of Horley, Surrey, to operate passenger-configured aircraft on eight-day inclusive-tours to Morrocco, and in 1982 one of these aircraft carried Club Mediterranee clients out of Dakar for a vacation in the Cape Verde Islands. Still in Africa, one Dakota was hired by Africair to carry out an Air Senegal contract, which lasted until April 1983. Back in the UK a lucrative three-year contract from the Ordnance Survey for photographic survey flights led to the establishment of a new subsidiary, Atlantic Surveys, and the modification of another Dakota to serve as backup to the already-equipped G-ANAF. This was the beginning of an association that was to continue throughout the lifetime of the Air Atlantique group. By the end of 1982 eight Dakotas were in service, alongside four Cessna 310 twins and one Cessna Citation corporate jet. The smaller aircraft were usually assigned to the air taxi flights, some of

The cover of a glossy brochure outlining the various operations offered by Air Atlantique in the early 1980s.

Cessna 310 G-SOUL at Jersey in June 2003, with Atlantic Flight Training titles on its wingtip fuel tanks. (Courtesy of Rosemary Ames)

Cessna Citation 1 G-LOFT was offered for executive charters and is seen here at the Coventry base. (Courtesy of Eric Melrose)

which transported Jersey residents to and from Switzerland, where they had business interests. Not all passenger charters were so glamorous. The shortest flight operated in 1982 covered just 14 air miles. A company boss wanted to arrive at his firm's Christmas lunch in style, so hired a Dakota to fly him into a nearby airfield where he disembarked in solitary splendour. More unusual Dakota charters transported a consignment of brandy from Cognac into the UK and carried a party of pig farmers from Aberdeen to Coventry, but it was the mail and newspaper contracts that provided vital year-round revenue. Three Dakotas were stationed at Blackpool for newspaper flights to Belfast and the Isle of Man, and two more carried mail between Newcastle and Liverpool on five nights each week. The Dakotas' large freight door and high-capacity ventilation system proved especially useful for livestock flights when a special penning system allowed loads in excess of 3,200 kg to be carried to most of Europe, Scandinavia and North Africa. The livestock included cattle, prize bulls, trotting horses, pigs and even a consignment of dolphins from Southampton to Lubeck in Germany. By the beginning of 1983 the Air Atlantique fleet had grown to some fifteen aircraft, based at Blackpool, Jersey, Newcastle and the Midlands. In January of that year Dakota G-AMSV and a crew under the command of former RAF Lightning pilot Paul Holroyd was despatched to the Sahara Desert for twenty-one days to act as support aircraft for the competitors in that year's Paris-Dakar motor rally. During this period they transported spare parts and supplies into desert airstrips such as Ourgla, Bordj, Omar Driss, Korhogo and El Golea. Other Dakota assignments that year carried day-old chicks to Zagreb, and a 2-tonne chandelier to North Africa.

On 6 June 1984 it was the 40th anniversary of the D-Day landings in Normandy. Many events were organised to commemorate the happenings on that date in 1944, including a day visit to the landing beaches for veterans, history buffs and the press, organised by this author. The arrangements originally called for a Dakota to fly into the airfield at Caen in Normandy, but shortly before the big day that airfield was commandeered by the military to accommodate government VIP flights, and so it transpired that on 6 June 1984 Air Atlantique's Dakota G-AMPO flew its load of veterans and local media out of Coventry

Oil-stained Dakota G-AMPO rests at Blackpool following an obvious problem with its port engine. (Courtesy of Mike Heap)

11

Dakota G-AMPY in an early version of the Air Atlantique livery at the Blackpool base. (Courtesy of Mike Heap)

Dakota G-AMSV in an unusual colour scheme at Blackpool. (Courtesy of Mike Heap)

Dakota G-ANAF wearing another version of the early candy-stripe livery. (Courtesy of Mike Heap)

Dakota G-APML, seen here at Blackpool, was rarely in active service during its time with Air Atlantique. (Courtesy of Mike Heap)

Dakota G-AMPY at the airline's Stansted base. (Glen Fricker)

and into Deauville instead. From there a coach took them around the landing beaches and other sites before eventually returning them to the airport. Unfortunately, severe road congestion along the route resulted in the party arriving back at Deauville much later than planned. The Dakota took off for Coventry, but halfway across the Channel the crew were informed that Coventry Airport would be closing for the night before they could get there, and consequently the Dakota had to land at Birmingham instead.

By June 1984 the original base at Jersey Airport had been outgrown, so it was decided to transfer all operations except the air taxi flights to the UK mainland. The cargo operations were relocated to Stansted and transferred to a new subsidiary, Atlantic Air Transport. In June 1984 the airline was operating night mail services along three routes. Flight DG201 connected Luton to East Midlands and Glasgow; DG202 was the return leg to Luton, but without the stop at East Midlands; and DG101 and DG102 were from Newcastle to Liverpool and return. On occasions it was not unusual for the three Dakotas engaged on

Dakota G-APML in the company's Stansted airport hangar. (Glen Fricker)

these services to all be in the vicinity of the Pole Hill radio beacon in Lancashire at around the same time. The Post Office mail contracts all had rigorous conditions attached, with penalties levied for late arrival of flights and more severe ones if the airline failed to operate the flight at all. This led to some challenging flights in marginal weather, including ice, snow, fog, strong winds and even St Elmo's Fire on occasions, but a great spirit of camaraderie was maintained between crews. By 1985 Air Atlantique had eight Dakotas in service and the group relocated once again, this time to Coventry Airport, which was to become the Air Atlantique group's permanent headquarters and operating base. One of the Dakotas that had joined the fleet was the former Martin-Baker aircraft G-APML, which was to remain a source of spares for the rest of its life and never flew for Air Atlantique. In April 1985 delays caused by adverse weather and engine problems led to Air Atlantique relinquishing the mail contracts and three Dakotas to a newly formed carrier, Air Luton. During that year two freshly overhauled Dakota engines were acquired from a new source and fitted to G-AMRA. These greatly reduced the delays caused by engine problems. The airline now concentrated on operating ad hoc charter flights and gradually built up the business again. As before, flexibility was the key, and unusual cargoes carried in October 1985 included a consignment of sheep from Le Havre to Belfast.

Meanwhile, things had not been going well for Air Luton. By the autumn of 1985 it was short of crews and had to sub-contract some of its flights back to Air Atlantique. In February 1986 Air Luton was obliged to hand over the mail contracts to another carrier, Topflight, with Air Atlantique overseeing the transfer. Topflight's operation of the mail flights was to last only a few weeks. The contract returned to Air Luton, but they eventually had to cease operations. One of the former Air Atlantique Dakotas, G-AMPO, later found its way back to them to become a source of spare parts for the five operational fleet members.

In order to try to convey some of the flavour of flying for Air Atlantique during this period I am pleased to paraphrase here some memories kindly supplied by Glen Fricker FRAeS.

Glen's 'interview' for a flying post consisted of a telephone conversation with Mike Collett on 14 June 1984, very soon after which he found himself travelling in the 'jump seat' of Dakota G-AMSV on a positioning flight from the airline's Stansted base to Southampton. On the next morning, a full load of aviation enthusiasts boarded the aircraft for a day trip to the RAF Cosford air show. After they had disembarked there the Dakota was kept busy operating pleasure flights from Cosford until it was time for the tired but happy enthusiasts to embark for the flight home. It was around this period that Glen sat a written examination on the workings of the Dakota, continuing his training until 27 June 1984 when he qualified as a First Officer with Air Atlantique. His first operation in this new position took the form of a flight from Stansted to Newcastle and back, sharing the flight deck with Captain Brian Knock. During his first nine months with the airline he also flew under the command of Captains Bill Scheerboom, Rick Seed, Paul Sabin, Paul Holroyd and Terry Bridle. Other Air Atlantique First Officers included Gordon Bennett, Andrew Dixon, Mike Collins and Gavin Wightman. The Operations Manager at that time was Colin Wright. Russell Warman was one of the hangar engineers. When passengers were carried, hostess duties were carried out by Nicky and Izzy. Debbie Frigot worked on the sales and marketing side. After renewing his Instrument Rating on 2 July 1984 Glen was rostered onto the mail flights to Glasgow. His logbook records several incidences of engine trouble during the latter half of 1984, including those affecting G-AMSV on 4 September, G-AMSY on 13 September, and G-ANAF on 26 and 31 October. During the autumn and winter of 1984 the Dakota crews were subject to recurrent 'base checks', during which various emergencies would be simulated in the course of a flight. For convenience, these would usually take place during the empty Stansted–Glasgow leg of a mail run. On one of these services Glen Fricker was aloft in G-AMCA on 20 December 1984. The Dakota was in the vicinity of Bradford when a real emergency developed. The starboard engine failed at a height of around 9,000 ft. The propeller of that engine was quickly feathered to reduce drag, but the aircraft continued to lose height. At 6,000 ft or so the decision was taken to turn back to Stansted, but a few minutes later the port engine also failed. A Mayday distress call was transmitted and the location of the nearest airport requested. The crew were advised that they were around 16 miles from the extended centreline of Runway 24 at Manchester. According to their calculations they only had enough altitude for another 8 miles or so of travel, but they pressed on for Manchester, all the while trying to restart at least one engine. To their great relief the port engine restarted when they were down to 2,500 ft and they were able to make a safe landing at Manchester. Investigations revealed that the fuel pipe to the carburettor on the starboard engine had fallen off and fuel had been pumping out of the tank in use for the port engine. On another occasion the crew were informed before departure that a Civil Aviation Authority inspector would be accompanying them throughout to check that all compulsory procedures were being adhered to. During the preflight inspection a small tear was discovered in the fabric on one elevator, and the crew assumed that the inspector would ground the aircraft until the fault had been fixed. To their surprise, he suggested that a patch of gaffer tape should do the trick, and after this had been applied he signed the aircraft off as fit for service. Crews on the mail run to Glasgow took great care to make their ground time there as comfortable as possible. Air Atlantique had acquired a four-bedroom house in Clarkston, near Glasgow, and an old Mini Clubman car for use by crews during stopovers. After arriving at Glasgow, usually at around 0100 hrs, the northbound crew could use this vehicle to get to the house. Supplies of food, beer and videos were kept there, and after a sleep it would be someone's job to replenish these at the local supermarket. The rest of the day was free until the crew reported for duty at the airport for the southbound leg to Luton, which usually landed there at around 0030 hrs. At weekends, however, Air Atlantique had no mail flights rostered and so the crew of the Friday northbound service would normally hitch a ride back down south on another carrier's service, a procedure known as 'Skyhiking'. This practice was applied on a reciprocal basis by the various airlines on the mail contracts. Using this method it was usually possible for the crew to arrive into Stansted Airport very early on a Saturday morning, either on an Air Bridge Carriers Merchantman freighter or occasionally on a Jersey European Airways Twin Otter aircraft. The facilities available in crew rooms varied between airports. At East Midlands a cup of coffee could be made between flights, while Liverpool Airport was considered to be superior, with a pleasant area offering coffee and soup on Monday to Thursday nights and even curry on Fridays. At the other end of the route, some of the Air Atlantique staff shared the accommodation at Brown End Cottage, another company house around half a mile from Stansted Airport. This building was still standing in 2019, but the company's hangar at Stansted was pulled down in the late 1980s. In December 1985 the staff Christmas party was held in Jersey, and Colin Wright managed to juggle the flying rosters so that all the aircrew would be free to attend. Glen Fricker was away in Europe with Andrew Dixon on a week-long 'round-robin' Ford charter, but was able to make it to Jersey with the aid of an aircraft change. Charter flights utilising the Bristol 170 and another Dakota were also rearranged so that their crews would be in Jersey on that date. Glen Fricker made his last flight for Air Atlantique on 16 August 1987, bringing Dakota G-AMSV back from an air show at Baldonnell in Ireland with Mike Collett.

On 11 November 1986 Dakota G-AMCA was rolled out at Exeter after a repaint into the airline's new livery of grey, green and white. Still to be applied was a new tail fin logo, the design of which was to be decided after a competition open to staff and customers. The winning entry, which featured an osprey clutching a fish in its talons, was first unveiled during the summer of 1987. By late 1986 Air Atlantique had developed a lucrative network of cargo routes, mainly on behalf of the Ford Motor Company. During a typical week an aircraft would fly from Coventry to Southampton and onwards to Cologne. After a night stop it would continue onwards to Valencia and another overnight stop. The itinerary continued in this pattern until arrival back at Coventry on the Friday evening. During night stops the crews were usually accommodated in four-star hotels. More unusual one-off cargoes carried by the Dakotas that year included: A party of thirty journalists from Northolt to Barrow-in-Furness to cover the launching of a new submarine at the Vickers works; bulk supplies of the British Gas privatisation prospectus from Stansted to Cardiff and from Gatwick and Norwich to the Channel Islands; and an ITN television crew, plus a portable transmitter and satellite dish, from Luton to Sumburgh and back.

A visitor to the Coventry base around the end of 1986 could have been forgiven for gaining the impression that most of the staff there had at least two jobs. Freight Manager Issy Henderson and the airline's Passenger Manager Deborah Frigot also looked after PR duties, and when passengers were to be transported they donned uniform and became stewardesses. Issy Henderson also did a long stint as editor of the airline's newsletter *Atlantique Antics*. Even the company MD James Foden was a skilled engineer, and also carried out piloting duties when necessary. One day in December 1986 Dakota G-AMRA was being loaded at Liverpool with a consignment of 3,500 kg of fruit and vegetables bound for the Isle of Man. At the last minute the consignor asked if he could add 'a few more cabbages' to the load. The crew noticed that the aircraft responded sluggishly to the controls while taxiing but proceeded with the take-off. They then realised that it was taking a lot of effort to raise the tail into the flying position, and by the time this was accomplished it was too late to abandon the take-off. The Dakota finally left the ground after full nose-down trim was applied. Once the aircraft had reached a safe airspeed and altitude the First Officer went back into the cabin to investigate and found several boxes stowed beyond the aft centre of gravity limit. He spent much of the flight dragging some of the cargo forward, and a cautious landing was safely made on the Isle of Man. After the consignment had been offloaded and weighed it was found that the aircraft had been around 1.5 tonnes overweight, and all of its cargo had been stowed well aft of the correct position.

Although Air Atlantique's association with four-engined DC-6 aircraft in 1979 had been short-lived, the acquisition of two more of the type in 1987 proved much more successful. These particular aircraft were the DC-6A cargo variant and were among the last examples to roll off the Douglas production line. One of them, to be registered as G-SIXC, was

Dakota G-AMCA displays the new 1986 livery – minus the tail logo, which was still to be decided upon.

Dakota G-AMRA in the full 1986 livery, complete with osprey tail logo.

Dakota G-AMPZ in the livery adopted in 1986.

purchased from Trans-Continental Airlines in the USA for the sum of US$650,000, which included US$170,000 to cover the cost of the modifications needed to re-register it in the UK. It's previous role had been transporting automobile components, and it was to continue this work, along with other duties, during its time with Air Atlantique. In late 1986 eight engineers had been sent across to the USA to prepare the aircraft for its ferry flight to the UK and to undergo training on the type. Paul Sabin, James Foden and five Air Atlantique Dakota pilots attended a two-week aircrew conversion course with DC-6 operator Trans Air Link at Miami in January 1987. On 22 March 1987 the aircraft set off from Willow Run Airport in Detroit on the first stage of its 14 hr 20 min delivery flight. After an overnight stop at Gander in Newfoundland the aircraft took off on the final stage of its journey to the UK. Before delivery it had been repainted in Air Atlantique's new green and white livery with the exception of the tail fin logo, which was still under discussion. Upon arrival in the Midlands the DC-6A performed a fly-past at Birmingham Airport before landing at its new Coventry airport base. The aircraft was officially welcomed to its new home by the mayor of Coventry, with a champagne reception held on 2 April 1987. Later that month it entered commercial service with a newspaper flight from Manchester to Dublin. The second example was obtained on lease from a Hong Kong-based company and had spent a considerable time in outside storage in the Yemen. After restoration to flying condition it was ferried by a crew under the command of James Foden to Southend

19

Douglas DC-6A G-SIXC during its delivery flight from the USA in 1987.

Airport, arriving there on 26 April 1987. Here it spent the remainder of that year, being overhauled by Heavylift and regaining the UK registration G-APSA it had carried while with British Eagle International Airlines. It entered service being flown on behalf of the Instone Airline Co. by Air Atlantique and carrying the titles of both airlines. In March 1989 it went on long-term lease from Instone to Air Atlantique, but the Instone name was still carried on the tail fin for the time being. In the interests of commonality with the Dakota fleet, the Twin Wasp engines of the DC-6As were modified to run on 100-octane unleaded gasoline – a lower rating than specified when the aircraft were new. The aircraft's payload was in the region of 13.5 tons. Few concessions were made to crew comfort. As the DC-6As normally cruised at altitudes of 6,000–8,000 ft they were operated unpressurised, with oxygen masks being carried for use when necessary. No autopilot was fitted and no loadmaster was carried; the Flight Engineer was expected to perform those duties. In the early 1990s the airline was quoting a flat rate of £2,200 per hour for international flights using the DC-6As, with domestic flights being charged at 'a little more'. Out of the ordinary DC-6As sorties saw G-SIXC flying cargo to Baghdad via Istanbul, and the type also visited the Faroe Islands, as did the Dakotas.

DC-6A G-APSA during its time when operated by Air Atlantique on behalf of the Instone Airline Co.

DC-6A G-APSA at Coventry in the hybrid Air Atlantique/Instone Airline livery.

A sticker issued to promote Air Atlantique's DC-6A freight services.

The year 1987 was also a significant one for Air Atlantique as it was awarded a five-year (later extended to seven-year) contract by the UK Department of Transport for the provision of marine pollution control services. This contract required the fleet to be almost doubled – to seventeen aircraft – by 1 November that year. Two more Dakotas and five Britten-Norman Islanders would have to be acquired and fitted with aerial spraying equipment, and a Cessna 402 would have to equipped for remote sensing surveillance using specialised equipment, including Ericsson sideways scanning radar. The original terms of the contract called for seven sprayer-equipped Dakotas to be kept on short-notice standby, but this was later revised to just two of these aircraft. The contract fleet was

The DC-6As roamed far and wide on cargo services. G-SIXC is seen here at Istanbul in March 1989. (Courtesy of Simon Brooke)

DC-6A G-SIXC awaits its load alongside an Iraqui Airways Boeing 707 at Baghdad in March 1989. (Courtesy of Simon Brooke)

The cargo-configured DC-6A G-APSA.

Atlantic Cargo DC-6A G-APSA taxies in after arrival in the Faroe Islands. (Courtesy of Frooi Poulsen)

Atlantic Cargo DC-6A G-APSA on a wintry taxiway in the Faroe Islands. (Courtesy of Frooi Poulsen)

Dakota G-AMRA sits on an icy ramp in the Faroe Islands. (Courtesy of Frooi Poulsen)

Dakota G-AMRA during a cargo sortie to the Faroe Islands. (Courtesy of Frooi Poulsen)

originally to be dispersed around the UK, with two sprayer Dakotas plus the Cessna 402 based at Coventry, two of the Islanders in Scotland, one more at Lydd Airport in Kent, and a further example at Exeter. During the summer of 1987 Dakota G-AMCA was ferried across the Atlantic to Greybull, Wyoming, via Godthaab in Greenland, Iqaluit, North West Territories and Winnipeg for installation of its spraying gear, returning to the UK to act as a pattern aircraft for the modification of the other Dakotas in-house. For the spring of 1988 Dakotas G-AMPY, G-AMRA and G-AMSV were configured for freight or passenger charters, with G-AMCA and G-AMHJ equipped and ready for pollution-spraying duties. The dispersant was pumped out at a rate of almost 200 gal/min through spray bars attached to the rear fuselage, with the apparatus being driven by an air turbine installed under the fuselage.

The Dakotas were still available for last-minute duties, including stepping in to take over mail runs when the regular aircraft became unserviceable. During the late 1980s and 1990s, for example, Exeter Airport was linked into the mail network, with Jersey European Airways Short 360s bringing in mail from Liverpool and flights back to Liverpool being operated by Channel Express Herald turbo-props, but when any of these aircraft failed Air Atlantique Dakotas were frequently substituted at short notice. In 1988 Air Atlantique's fleet of Dakotas was instrumental in the airline recording a profit of £1.9 million. Mike Collett predicted that the type was good for at least another fifty years of flying, and perhaps more if the fleet was re-engined with PT6 turbo-props. In the late 1980s the Air Atlantique crew roster included the following pilots:

Dakota Captains: David Cuthbert (Jersey), Ian Stait (Jersey)
DC-6 Captains: James Foden, Vic Surrage
DC-6 First Officers: Malcolm Scott, Ron Keyte, Terry Maskell (Coventry)
Multi-type rated First Officers: John Graham (DC-6, Dakota, Cessna 310; Jersey), John Fryderburg (DC-6, Piper Aztec; Jersey)

Dakota G-AMCA, one of several assigned to the Department of Transport Pollution Control contract. (Courtesy of Eric Melrose)

Dakota G-AMCA at Godthaab/Nuuk airport in Greenland during its trip to Wyoming in August 1987 for installation of spraying equipment. (Courtesy of Simon Brooke)

Dakota G-AMCA transits at Igaluit, NW Territories, Canada, in August 1987. (Courtesy of Simon Brooke)

Dakota G-AMCA refuels at Winnipeg in August 1987. (Courtesy of Simon Brooke)

Dakota G-AMRA at Exeter during a tight night mail schedule. (Courtesy of Tony Perry)

Some of the many liveries worn by Dakota G-ANAF during its service with the Air Atlantique group. (Courtesy of Will Jarman)

Never a company to stand still for long, Air Atlantique diversified its activities once again in May 1988, this time venturing into the field of scheduled passenger services. A five-times daily schedule between Southampton and the Channel Islands was launched using a single HS-748 turbo-prop twin – the much-travelled G-BEKG. Long before the coming of easyJet and the like, Air Atlantique advertised itself as 'Britain's first direct-sell airline', as it was not going to sell its tickets through travel agents. With the aid of an attractive one-way fare of £29, the airline succeeded in selling more than 20,000 seats during its first month of operation, prompting it to announce its intention to introduce larger turbo-prop equipment such as the Dash 8, ATP or ATR 42/72 in the future. However, it soon felt the impact of competition from the much better-known Air UK and its established network of travel agents and was forced to rethink its policy and use the travel trade to fill its flights during the lean winter season. Even so, in 1988 it incurred losses of £750,000 on its Channel Island scheduled services. From 1990 onwards the Channel Islands routes were operated under by a new subsidiary named Air Corbiere. New routes were introduced in subsequent years, including daily flights linking the Channel Islands with Coventry and Gloucester/Staverton in June 1991, and daily services from Jersey and Guernsey to Rennes in northern France June 1992. That

HS 748 G-BEKG, used on scheduled services to the Channel Islands in 1988.

same month daily services linking Liverpool with the Channel Islands were launched, sometimes using the HS-748 but often using the airline's Metro III aircraft. When not rostered on scheduled services, this twin-engined turbo-prop was available for ad hoc charters, for which its capacity of nineteen passengers or over 2 tonnes of cargo proved very attractive.

During 1989 the surveillance Cessna 402 was flying some 30–35 hrs each month on pollution-patrol duties – around half of its total usage. On 12 May 1990 the entire pollution-control fleet was detached to Exeter Airport, where a large oil tanker had collided with a Brixham trawler and an oil slick had appeared off the south coast of Devon. This was successfully dealt with, and all the aircraft returned to their bases on the afternoon of 14 May.

By 1990 many of the DC-6A flights were being operated on behalf of other airlines. On 28 June 1990 G-SIXC was chartered by Lufthansa for an early morning Manchester–Frankfurt cargo service. Once unloaded there, the aircraft was ferried to Birmingham in preparation for a cargo flight to Turin and after this operation it was positioned to Liverpool in readiness for its next sortie. The other example, G-APSA, was also kept busy on sub-contract work. During the early hours of 2 August 1990, it operated a Manchester–Frankfurt cargo service for the German national airline Lufthansa. After unloading there it assumed an Aer Lingus callsign for a Frankfurt–Dublin cargo service as 'Shamrock 9658'. For the winter 1990/1 season Air Atlantique's charter fleet consisted of the two DC-6As and the Dakota G-AMRA. On 6 April 1992 Air Atlantique began the operation of a contract with

The versatile Fairchild Metro III G-BUKA, also used by Air Corbiere on Channel Islands services.

The very tidy flight deck of Dakota G-AMRA.

Air Express International for a nightly freight service between Coventry and Brussels. On this run the DC-6As cruised at around 300 mph and had a range with maximum payload in the region of 3,000 miles. The AEI contract provided the first regular work for these aircraft, their previous flights having been on a one-off, ad hoc basis. The first service was operated as flight AAG801 by G-SIXC, with G-APSA on standby as a reserve aircraft. The turnround time at Brussels was usually in the region of 2 hrs 45 mins, and during the stopover the crew consumed refreshments they had brought with them, as no crew meals or vouchers were supplied by the airline. The pair of DC-6As soon became very busy, operating a total of ten sectors between them in a single day on 30 April 1992. An idea of the variety of routeings flown by the Dakota and DC-6A fleets during a typical winter season is provided in Appendix 3 of this book. By 1994 the DC-6As had also been contracted to carry newspapers between Liverpool and Dublin. The assigned aircraft was usually positioned empty from Coventry to Liverpool. Once the DC-6A was parked on its stand, 'dribble cans' were positioned under the engines to prevent the inevitable oil dribbles from staining the tarmac. The Liverpool–Dublin leg usually operated under flight number AAG851. After unloading at Dublin the aircraft was usually flown empty directly back to Coventry, occasionally carrying the odd express parcel consignment. In its marketing material Air Atlantique made a point of emphasising its ability to have an aircraft airborne within one hour of receiving an 'immediate' ad hoc charter request. The DC-6As and Dakotas were relatively cheap to acquire and maintain, allowing the airline to keep examples on standby for quick response. In a magazine interview in 1993, Mike Collett spelt out his fundamentals for making a profit using the DC-6As:

> Good maintenance, carried out by people who know the aircraft ... Pilots who are familiar with the aircraft and who, preferably, have not been spoiled by flying simple types with turbines ... A sensible management approach which does not ask more of the DC-6A than it is capable of giving ... and a sound commercial operation. There is not much future in being a sound operator with no work.

On 23 December 1992 fog played havoc with pre-Christmas services. Around fifteen passengers were booked to travel out to the Channel Islands with Air Corbiere, and twenty-eight holidaymakers were waiting to fly home from Jersey, but their allocated aircraft was fogbound elsewhere. The freighter Dakota G-AMPZ was hastily reconfigured for passenger carrying, the cabin was warmed up by heaters, and complimentary champagne was placed on board for the inconvenienced passengers. The Dakota carried the outbound passengers to Jersey, took returning holidaymakers on board and set off for Coventry. Unfortunately, as they neared, the airport was closed by fog and the Dakota diverted to Bristol. Here, the passengers booked to fly to Gloucester/Cheltenham and Coventry were transferred to coaches and the aircraft took off for Liverpool with the remaining fourteen. All of the affected passengers arrived home at the correct place in time for Christmas. In 1994 the Air Corbiere services to the Channel Islands were discontinued.

Another major oil spill response operation began on 5 January 1993 when Air Atlantique received a call from the government's Marine Pollution Control unit advising that the airline's assistance may shortly be needed. The oil tanker 'MV Braer' was adrift and apparently heading for Shetland. Cessna 402 and 404 surveillance aircraft were scrambled from Inverness and Coventry to assess the situation and the Inverness-based Dakotas G-AMPO and G-ANAF were brought to readiness. The decision was then taken to send Dakotas G-AMCA, G-AMHJ, G-AMPY and G-AMYJ north to join them. By early the next day all six Dakotas were on station at Sumburgh, Shetland, and took off to attack the oil slick, which had now appeared on the sea surface. Operating in winds of around 50 knots, they sprayed some 120 tons of dispersant that day. The Dakotas remained at Sumburgh for the next couple of days and were joined by the DC-6A G-SIXC, which had also been fitted with spraying equipment. However, the winds increased to hurricane strength and for a time the aircraft were grounded. The Dakotas were positioned behind improvised windbreaks of dispersant drums and sandbags were placed on their wing leading edges. By the Friday the conditions necessitated the withdrawal of the Dakotas to Inverness, but the following day was calmer and they returned to Sumburgh to recommence spraying, flying as low as 50 ft on a curving track leading towards a 900-ft cliff. The high winds helped to complete the dispersal of the slick and, even though the vessel broke up on the Monday night, a survey flight later reported no further significant pollution. After a further couple of days on standby the fleet was finally released to return to its various bases. By 2000 the management of this contract had passed to the Maritime and Coastguard Agency. In the event of an alert an Air Atlantique Cessna 404 (which had replaced the Cessna 402) was to carry out the initial reconnaissance, with a fully loaded sprayer aircraft ready to be overhead the scene within 6 hours.

Dakota G-AMHJ, another of the examples used on the Pollution Control contract. The spray bar is just visible, forward of the tailplane.

Air Atlantique Cessna 404 Titan G-EXEX parked on the grass at Jersey airport. (Courtesy of Rosemary Ames)

In 1990 Air Atlantique acquired the Malta-based Malta International Aviation Co., renaming it CFS Aeroproducts in 1995. Its engineering operations were transferred to the former Alvis factory on the perimeter of Coventry Airport. Here, freshly overhauled Pratt & Whitney R-2800 and R-1830 engines arrived from the USA and were prepared for installation in the airline's DC-6As and Dakotas, with two spare Dakota engines on permanent standby at Coventry. CFS became the Atlantic Group's engine and airframe contractor as well as carrying out overhauls on all sizes of piston engines, Allison turbo-prop engines, propellors and undercarriages for vintage warbirds such as Hurricanes, P-51 Mustangs and Harvards for operators throughout the world. At one stage a notice at the base proclaimed, 'If it burns and turns, bangs and blows, points, indicates, potentiates, or anything in-between, there's a good chance we can fix it.'

Despite its many commitments Air Atlantique was still able to take on unusual ad hoc charters, and on 9 August 1993 Dakota G-AMPZ transported the crew of a cable-laying vessel from Humberside to the island of Stord, off Norway. The runway there was under 1,000 m long, and the Dakota became the largest aircraft to land there at that time. On 1 September 1993 another Dakota, G-AMRA, was hired by Singapore International Airlines (SIA) to transport a party of award-winning travel agents from Stansted to Prestwick and back, operating under SIA flight numbers. In the summer of 1993, it looked like another propliner type might be joining the fleet when Air Atlantique successfully bid for the former South African Air Force Douglas DC-4 6907, but then promptly sold it on to an operator in Africa. In September 1993 Air Atlantique had nine Dakotas in service. Seven

Dakota G-ANAF sporting the large 'chin' radome carried during electronics trials for Racal. (Courtesy of Eric Melrose)

of these were committed to the oil-spill-spraying contract, for which the airline claimed a despatch reliability rate of better than 97 per cent. Dakota G-ANAF was assigned to a contract to carry out electronic trials work for Racal, and in connection with this it acquired a large 'chin' radome under its nose that it carried for many years.

In the autumn of 1993, the Atlantic Group comprised the following companies:

Air Atlantique

Ad hoc charter work with Dakota, DC-6A and Cessna Caravan II aircraft.

Atlantic Reconnaissance (later renamed RVL Aviation)

Provision of aircraft and crews for airborne remote sensing, survey and patrol duties, using Cessna Titan, Cessna Caravan II and Dakota aircraft equipped with SLR, infrared and UV sensors. Conversion of aircraft for these duties. This company had been established to take over responsibility for the fulfilment of the pollution control contracts and to carry out any future aerial survey work. In 1994 it was awarded a joint contract in conjunction with the

Marine Oil Spill Response Corporation of the USA for a surveillance and remote-sensing programme. For this work the Shorts 360 aircraft N360AR was fitted out at Coventry with pollution-detection sensors and highly sophisticated computer analysis and data-link equipment. In this configuration the aircraft participated in the 1994 Farnborough Air Show before departing to the USA for operations based at Ellington Field near Houston. In April 2007 the company was to be renamed RVL Aviation.

Atlantic Aeroengineering

Airframe and engine overhaul and repair. Special mission modifications.

Atlantic Flyers (later renamed Atlantic Flight Training)

Advanced flying training up to ATPL standard, tailored specifically to meet the demanding requirements of the Atlantic Group.

Aer Atlantic

Dublin-based 'quick reaction' ad hoc cargo and passenger flights using Shorts 360 and Piper Navajo aircraft. The General Manager was Paddy Kenny.

In August 1993 the aviation press was reporting that Richard Branson, the founder of Virgin Atlantic Airways, was understood to be in talks with Air Atlantique over the use of their Dakotas to operate 1940s-themed flights to Normandy or the Channel Islands from the south-east of England. The flights would be part of tours taking in historic sites from the Second World War and were said to have been inspired by the success of Mr Branson's Vintage Airtours Dakota flights between Orlando and Key West, which had commenced the previous year. In the end, the idea was not proceeded with.

By 1993 Air Atlantique was becoming concerned about the DC-6A's future ability to satisfy the regulations while operating at night into noise-sensitive airports such as Cologne, Frankfurt and Munich, and this led to the acquisition that summer of two Lockheed L-188 Electra turbo-prop aircraft to supplement and eventually replace them on flights into these airports. The Electra was the first turbo-prop airliner to be built in the USA and was powered by four Allison 501-D13 engines. It first flew in December 1957 and entered service with Eastern Airlines of the USA in January 1959. Up to ninety-eight passengers could be carried. The loss of three Electras in fatal accidents attributed to wing flutter between February 1959 and March 1960 all but ended the Electra's sales prospects, and production ended in 1961 after 170 had been constructed. Many were subsequently converted to freighters. Air Atlantique's first example of these 15-tonne capacity freighters was purchased in the USA and arrived at Coventry on 8 November 1993 after a delivery flight from Opa Locka, Florida, via Keflavik, Iceland. Re-registered as G-LOFA, this first Electra began operations in September 1993 on a four-nights-per-week Coventry–Brussels service. The airline intended to supplement this aircraft's efforts by using leased Electra

Lockheed Electra G-LOFB, wearing 'Atlantic' fuselage titles, on final approach to Jersey in May 1999. (Courtesy of Rosemary Ames)

N359Q, but apart from a training sortie from Coventry to Jersey and return on 18 November 1993 this aircraft remained hangar-bound at Coventry for much of December 1993 and January 1994. To replace the lost capacity Air Atlantique leased Electra N360Q from Renown Aviation in November 1993 at the termination of its lease to Channel Express. On 29 November this aircraft was ferried to Shannon in preparation for its first Air Atlantique operation – flight BCS966 from Shannon to East Midlands on behalf of Hunting Cargo Airlines. It was subsequently used by Air Atlantique on Hunting Cargo schedules from East Midlands to Shannon and Brussels until 18 January 1994 when it was ferried back to Coventry. During 1994, G-LOFA was despatched to Switzerland to operate contract parcel flights out of Basel. Air Atlantique's second Electra, G-LOFB, operated its first revenue service for the airline on 11 July 1994. Unlike the DC-6s the Electras carried a loadmaster on their flights, so were able to transport a payload of up to 15 tonnes over a distance of up to 2,200 miles, cruising at around 400 mph. On 30 July 1997, G-LOFA suffered an in-flight emergency while on a cargo service out of Berlin. It was passing through 15,000 ft with five crew members aboard when a sudden cabin decompression occurred. The aircraft was landed safely back at Berlin, where it was discovered that the main cargo door had blown open as a result of being improperly latched. Also, the appropriate warning light had been dimmed to a level where it could not be easily seen when illuminated.

In 1994 another group reorganisation took place. The name of the holding company became Atlantic Holdings Ltd, although it was generally referred to as the Atlantic Group. One reason for this name change was to avoid confusion with a French airline also called

Air Atlantique, which had been set up in 1976. The cargo operations of Air Atlantique and Air Corbiere were grouped together under the Atlantic Cargo name, while their passenger services and the air taxi operations traded under the Atlantic Airways name. However, all Dakota-operated services, pleasure flights and pollution control contract work still used the Air Atlantique name. Another subsidiary was Air Alba, which had been set up at Inverness airport in 1990 by Air Atlantique Chief Pilot Alan Mossman. By 1995 the company had the distinction of being the most northerly-based charter operator in the UK, and its roster of aircrew included Linton Chilcott, a former RAF Leuchars-based F-4 Phantom pilot. The company's activities that year included flying training as well as charter flights to remote parts of the Highlands, the Faroes and Scandinavia. Frequent flights were made to the beach airstrip on Barra using a Cessna 310 or a BN-2 Islander twin-engined aircraft. Every alternate Wednesday that year flights were operated from Benbecula to the remote island of St Kilda, bringing mail for the isolated army detachment there. As the island possessed no runway the mailbags were dropped by a despatcher in the rear seat as the aircraft flew over at low level. The company also operated tourist flights to the islands of Mull and Islay with five-seat Cessna 310s, and the Air Atlantique Cessna 402 G-EYES was used to transport shellfish from the Outer Hebrides to the Scottish mainland. Birdwatchers were also carried from Kirkwall, Orkney to Fair Isle in the Islander G-BNXA. In 1995 the Cessna 402 was replaced by Cessna 404 G-EXEX. This aircraft was assigned to maritime patrol work, usually around the rigs in the East Shetland Basin. Its missions could take up to 6 hours, and for them the Cessna was equipped with Sideways Looking Aircraft Radar, mounted beneath the front fuselage. In 1996 the management of the two Inverness-based Air Atlantique Dakotas was also entrusted to Air Alba. In February 1997 Air Alba was renamed Highland Airways and began to develop a scheduled services network. On 1 December that year an

Cessna 406 G-LEAF, wearing International Test Pilots School titles on its long nose. (Courtesy of Eric Melrose)

Highland Airways Jetstream 31 G-JURA on a visit to Aberdeen in May 2003.

This Christmas card commemorates, in seasonal style, the delivery of the group's first ATR-42 aircraft. (Courtesy of Will Jarman)

Aberdeen–Inverness freight and mail service was inaugurated, using a Cessna 406 aircraft. In 1998 the airline was awarded a contract to operate newspaper distribution flights out of Inverness on a twice-daily basis. For these flights Jetstream 31 turbo-prop aircraft were acquired In September 2001 Highland Airways commenced its 'Islander Hopper' passenger service between Stornoway and Benbecula, with connections provided between Inverness and Stornoway. This service was operated twice-daily on weekdays under a government Public Service Obligation (PSO) subsidised contract, using an eighteen-seat Jetstream 31 turbo-prop. The same type of aircraft was also used to operate regular flights between Glasgow and Filton, transporting BAe Systems staff between its establishments in these places. Another PSO contract was awarded for services between Anglesey and Cardiff, for which an aircraft was stationed in Wales. Additional work came with the awarding of another valuable contract, this time from the Scottish Fisheries Protection Agency for the provision of two Cessna 406 aircraft, crews and maintenance for reconnaissance duties for a five-year term. In subsequent years Highland Airways progressed to the acquisition of larger ATR-42 and ATR-72 turbo-props. The first ATR 42 to be acquired, a convertible passenger/cargo srs 300, joined the fleet in 2003. Two more examples followed in 2004 and 2005, and in 2005 and 2006 two of the larger ATR-72 models were also acquired. These turbo-props were not assigned exclusively to Highland Airways, but were also available for use by other companies in the group as traffic demand required. In March 2007 the Highland Airways CEO Alan Mossman led a successful management buyout, aided by a £620,000 investment from the Highlands and Islands Enterprise Development Agency, but in 2010 concerns over the airline's financial stability led to its closure and liquidation that year.

ATR-42 G-IONA on final approach.

On 15 February 1996 the Air Atlantique pollution control fleet was called into action once again. The 147,000-tonne supertanker *Sea Empress* had run aground off St Anne's Head, near Milford Haven, and an oil slick was developing. An Air Atlantique survey Cessna 404 was overhead the scene within 2 hours of the call, and by the following day all seven of the sprayer-configured Dakotas, plus another Cessna 404, had been flown into Haverfordwest airfield in south Wales. Each Dakota could carry 4.5 tonnes of dispersant, but they were could not go straight into action as they were not authorised to spray the dispersant within 1 km of land. A change in the wind and tide situation eventually allowed them to go ahead and successful spray runs were carried out, with the Dakotas operating at heights down to 15–20 feet above the waves.

In 1996 Atlantic Aero Engineering was tasked by the Dutch Dakota Association (DDA) with the technical support of its latest acquisitions, the Dakotas PH-DDZ and PH-PBA. The latter aircraft had previously served as the personal transport of HRH Prince Bernhard of the Netherlands, who was the patron of the DDA. After restoration it finally departed Coventry for the Netherlands on 4 November 1998. Other work entrusted to Atlantic Aero Engineering included annual checks on the two Douglas DC-4s that the DDA acquired from the South African Air Force, and the maintenance of the Berlin Airlift Historical Foundation's MATS-liveried Douglas C-54E 90414, *Spirit of Freedom*, during its European tour. In future years the company's unrivalled experience in the care of 'propliners' was to

The Dutch Dakota Association's Dakota PH-PBA, in for overhaul at Coventry in 1996. (Courtesy of Eric Melrose)

lead to its selection for the overhaul of the larger members of the Battle of Britain Memorial Flight. Dakota ZA947 received attention during the winter of 2005/6, and Lancaster PA474 arrived at Coventry for overhaul on 2 October 2006. In 1997 the Instone Air Lines interest in DC-6A G-APSA passed to the Air Atlantique Group, and the aircraft was registered to Atlantic Air Transport on 3 December 1997. The Air Atlantique Group was now 100 per cent owned by Atlantic Holdings and had 200 employees. Its subsidiaries now also included Portugal-based Aeronortec and Miami-based North American Turbine Services. Thanks to its extensive engineering resources at Coventry the group was now self-sufficient in the maintenance of its fleet. In June 1998 the Atlantic Group diversified still further when it took a 150-year lease on Coventry Airport and set up West Midlands International Airport Ltd to operate it. Appointed to the post of Airport Director was Peter Jackson, a former airline captain with experience on such types as the VC-10 and the Boeing 747, who had been a CAA aerodrome inspector for two years.

In 1999 Atlantic Cargo became the first UK operator of the Lockheed Electra in the Public Transport category to be authorised by the Civil Aviation Authority for two-pilot operations with the type. That year the Electra fleet recorded a technical despatch reliability (departures within 15 minutes of schedule) of 99.4 per cent. Another new type arrived at Coventry in May 2000 in the shape of Convair 440 CS-TML. Over 160 examples of this development of the Convair 240 and 340 had been built, powered by

Electra G-FIJR taxies in at Coventry during August 1998.

two Pratt & Whitney R-2800-CB16 piston engines and pressurised to carry up to fifty-two passengers. The type was intended to replace the Dakota in service, but faced competition from emerging turbo-prop transports such as the Vickers Viscount. Air Atlantique only operated this one Convair 440, which had been acquired from the Portuguese carrier Agro Air the previous year and came equipped with a side cargo door and a 6.5-ton payload capacity. It initially entered service wearing its Portuguese registration and titles, and between August and October 2000 carried cargo on routeings that included Coventry-Oporto, Coventry-Saarbrucken, Southend-Teeside and Teeside-Zaragoza. It was later allocated the UK registration G-CONV and was repainted in Air Atlantique livery and titles, but during a test flight for its UK Certificate of Airworthiness it suffered a fire in its port engine. This resulted in it being grounded at Coventry and eventually sold. By May 2000 Atlantic Cargo was operating seven Electras – the world's largest active fleet at that time – and had decided that the type would form the backbone of its cargo operations for at least the next ten years. That year, out of a total of fifty-four pilots, twenty-two were qualified on the Electra, and the Electra fleet averaged 80 flight hours each month. The DC-6As and freighter Dakotas flew around 500 hours that year. Utilisation of the two DC-6As was now becoming more problematical because of noise restrictions and the limited supply of Avgas fuel away from the Coventry base. With its 15-ton fuel capacity a DC-6A could uplift a year's supply of the scarce fuel in one refuelling at some airfields. Looking to the future, the airline was planning to expand the Electra fleet to a total of nine. Two more had already been acquired from the Norwegian carrier Fred Olsen Airtransport and, as the average age of the aircraft was around forty years, Air Atlantique was investing US$500,000 to update and extend the life of the fleet. In a magazine article Managing Director Russell Ladkin outlined the rationale behind the airline's unusual aircraft procurement policy:

We operate old aircraft because they make us money. Ad hoc cargo charters account for 90 per cent of our business, which means that our aircraft can often spend long periods inactive. So, it is vital to keep the fixed cost base as low as possible. This is what makes a forty-year old Electra better economically for Atlantic than a five-ten year old Boeing 737-300QC. We can acquire a good Electra for US$2 million, while a good 737 would trade for around US$20-30 million. You need high utilisation to cover those sort of purchase costs, which is not the nature of our business.

Someone purchasing a 737 today would reasonably expect to get 4000hrs annual utilisation out of it. We could only reckon on getting six or seven hundred hours out of it. Older aircraft are very labour-intensive, but their much lower initial cost makes sense for us. We can see at least another ten years of life in our Electras. However, we said that about the DC-6As in the late 1980s and we still have no plans to phase them out.

By then the Electras had already been modified and recertificated for two-crew operation. Under a modified maintenance schedule negotiated with the Civil Aviation Authority the interval between their checks had been reduced from 100 hours to 80 hours. Limited technical support for the Electras was still provided by Lockheed, but this no longer included the provision of spare parts, so the Atlantic Group set up Coventry Air Parts to

Air Atlantique's unlucky Convair 440 G-CONV, seen grounded at Coventry in 2003.

Atlantic Airlines Electra G-FIJV on a damp day at Aberdeen.

Atlantic Airlines Electra G-LOFD rests at Aberdeen between parcels contract flights.

procure and supply spares for in-house use and for sale to third-party operators. Small parts such as stringers could be fabricated in-house, while other parts could be obtained from suppliers such as the California-based Electra specialist Capco. New regulations were to be met by the installation of traffic alert and collision avoidance systems, and GPS was to be installed in two examples to equip them for transatlantic operations. This enabled the aircraft to undertake trips such as that operated by G-FIJR on 8 November 2000, flying from Coventry to Goose Bay, Labrador, and returning two days later. On the 18th of that month Electra G-LOFB also flew to Goose Bay and was back at Coventry on the evening of the following day. After refuelling and a crew change the aircraft was airborne again just after midnight, this time heading for Lisbon. More challenging sorties for the Electra fleet soon followed. On 14 December 2000 G-LOFE flew from Coventry to Baku in 6 and a half hours, returning the next day. On 22 January 2001 G-FIJR operated a freight charter to Rio De Janeiro via Las Palmas, Dakar (where a fresh crew took over) and Recife. After a 36-hour stopover in Rio the Electra returned empty to Coventry via Recife and Sal Island, with the whole trip taking 36 hours of flying time. For the winter of 2000/1 four Electras were flying under contract to carriers such as DHL and TNT, and three more examples were on standby for ad hoc charters. During the 1990s thought had been given to the acquisition of jet freighters and types such as the Boeing 727 and McDonnell Douglas DC-9 were considered, with the DC-8-70 on the long-term agenda. In May 2000 an L-100 commercial Hercules was leased in from Safair on a short-term basis. This aircraft could also be converted for spraying, with a large dispersant tank in the main cabin area and spraying booms that could be deployed from the lowered ramp at the rear.

Ever on the lookout for new ways of attracting traffic to its airport, in early 2000 the Atlantic Group installed a 5.5-degree PAPI glideslope system on Runway 23 at Coventry. This unusually steep approach angle was identical to the one in use at London City Airport, and the group made attempts to persuade BAe 146 and BAe RJ operators to use Coventry's uncongested airspace for training their pilots in carrying out approaches to London City. By then Atlantic Flight Training was providing the training for most of the new pilots recruited for the group. Candidates accepted for airline training joined as Cadets, and in between instruction periods they were expected to turn their hands to whatever odd jobs needed doing, such as cleaning aircraft, cutting the grass and working shifts in Operations. The upside of this was the fast-track promotion possible within the group, with many former cadets having graduated to command positions.

In May 2003, the DC-6As were still earning their keep on regular freight runs from Coventry to Saarbrucken and Zweibruken, but they were nearing the end of their time on commercial operations. G-APSA returned from Zweibruken to Coventry on its last commercial service on 23 September 2004, and G-SIXC ended its commercial service on 26 October that year with a flight from Gothenburg to Coventry. Both DC-6As were then placed into storage, but were later to re-emerge at Coventry in new roles. In March 2001, the trading activities of Atlantic Airlines were the subject of a management buyout led by the airline's Chief Executive Tony Auld and its Managing Director Russell Ladkin. The buyout was completed on 28 May 2004 when all the other assets, such as aircraft and spares, were also purchased from Air Atlantique. In January 2006, Atlantic Airlines took delivery of the first of five freighter conversions of the British Aerospace ATP twin-engined turbo-prop aircraft. Their story went back to 2000, when most of the passenger-configured ATPs sold had been returned to BAe, which had formed a division to lease them out to other carriers. In June of that year the renamed BAe Systems Group announced the launch of a freighter conversion programme for the aircraft. The programme was to be undertaken in partnership with the cargo airline West Air Sweden, who were already operating BAe 748s converted to carry freight. BAe was to design the sliding cargo doors, which West Air would fabricate and fit. By 2001 West Air was operating partially converted ATPs on overnight freight schedules, and on 10 July 2002 the first fully converted ATP freighter made its maiden flight from the West Air facility in Sweden. Atlantic Airlines saw the potential of this programme and ordered five conversions, taking delivery of the first example in January 2006. In February 2007 there followed by an agreement with BAe Systems Regional Aircraft for the long-term lease of further examples. In the meantime, the Electras continued to provide reliable service, and six remained in service in the summer of 2007. By then the management buyout of Atlantic Airlines had been completed, but a resume of the company's following operations may be of interest. Two Electras operated on behalf of TNT on flights out of Liege to destinations such as Cardiff, Edinburgh, Liverpool and Nurenburg. G-LOFE was stationed in Copenhagen, operating for DHL, and the other three were used on Coventry–Belfast freight runs and Jersey–Bournemouth mail services. Ad hoc charters were still fitted in during 2007. On 14 September G-LOFC operated a multi-sector charter that routed Shannon–Wroclaw–Vitoria–Coventry; on 10 October G-LOFB flew Coventry–Pescara–Valladolid–Bournemouth; and on 7 December G-FIZU operated from Belfast to Ankara via Doncaster, flying back from Ankara to Liverpool on the following

Atlantic Airlines BAe ATP G-BTPH at Aberdeen in July 2006.

Atlantic Airlines BAe ATP G-BUUR at Aberdeen on a misty day in April 2009.

day. Atlantic Airlines did not retire its last Electra until early 2013. This aircraft had been operating daily flights between Leipzig and Katowice for DHL, and after its last service and after checks at Coventry it was ferried to Canada to join the Electra fleet of Buffalo Airways. In total, eleven examples had served with Air Atlantique/Atlantic Airlines. In 2015 the Atlantic Airlines fleet of seventeen turbo-props was transferred onto the Swedish Air Operators Certificate of the West Atlantic Group and the aircraft were re-registered in Sweden. On 1 November 2017, the airline name was officially changed to West Atlantic UK Ltd. By 2019 the ATPs had been almost totally superseded by Boeing 737 freighters.

3

Showtime

Right from their introduction the nostalgic sight and sound of Air Atlantique's Dakotas and DC-6As going about their business attracted interest from aviation enthusiasts and the general public alike, and it soon became apparent that large numbers of people would be only too keen to pay to see these aircraft up close and to ride in them at air shows and open days. The airline's founder, Mike Collett, was an enthusiast and was keen to share his passion for vintage aircraft with like-minded people who could provide revenue to keep them flying, and so a new era began. During the summer of 1981 some 6,000 passengers were carried aloft on pleasure flights at air shows, and in May 1983 G-AMPO carried out a season of pleasure flights at events that included the RAF Innsworth Open Day at Staverton Airport, the Biggin Hill Air Fair, the RAF Coltishall Open Day, and the North Weald Military Display. These flights continued for many years but were not always without incident. On 25 July 1984 one of the Dakotas was operating pleasure flights out of RAF Brawdy. During one of these sorties a supercharger drive shaft split. As the passengers disembarked afterwards, one of them came up to the flight deck and asked the crew if they were aware that there was oil all over the port wing. They were not, and after efforts to remedy the fault followed by a couple of engine runs the problem still persisted. The crew did not want to be stranded at Brawdy with their sick aircraft and so decided to take off with both engines running. Once out of sight from the airfield they would shut down the ailing powerplant for the remainder of the journey to Exeter. Carrying out this plan involved diplomatically declining the offer of a Hawker Hunter escort for part of the way and hoping no one would be too alarmed by their smoky departure. A few weeks after that G-AMRA and two other Dakotas were positioned to West Malling airfield to participate in an air show over the weekend of 26/27 August. Their role was to drop a large contingent of parachutists onto the airfield. After a downwind run to assess the wind strength and direction the Dakotas turned back towards the airfield, at which point the jump-master aboard G-AMRA made an unplanned departure through the open-door aperture. Fortunately, he was wearing his parachute and came to earth unharmed, but some of the other jumpers thought they were meant to follow him and also jumped, landing quite a long way from the airfield. On many of these positioning flights the passengers obtained their tickets through the 'Friends of the DC-3', and they became familiar faces to

Promotional 'Fly The Dakota'
sticker issued during the
pleasure flying era.

Air Atlantique DC-6A G-SIXC on show in the static park at the International Air Tattoo at RAF
Fairford in 1991.

DC-6A G-SIXC climbs out to start its display at the 1994 Woodford Air Show.

DC-6A G-SIXC performs a fly-past with 'everything down' at the Woodford Air Show in 1994.

DC-6A G-SIXC lands after its display at the Woodford Air Show in 1994.

Examples of ticket covers issued for passenger charters/pleasure flights.

PASSENGER TICKET AND BAGGAGE CHECK

Please read important notice on page six

Air Atlantique

This ticket is issued by Air Atlantique, subject to the Company's Conditions of Carriage for Passenger and Baggage, Regulations, Timetables and Notices, which may be inspected at the Company's office

Dakota G-AMPY in period Northwest Airlines livery, applied to commemorate that airline's 60th anniversary.

54

the crews. This led to quite a few pranks being played on them by the crews as a way of enlivening the journey. These included leaving the flight-deck door wide open, so that the passengers could see and hear the pilots heatedly discussing the map on their knees with puzzled expressions. Another favourite trick involved two lengths of elastic, which they attached to suitable points within the cockpit. One pilot would then back out of the flight deck with one of the lengths in each hand. He would stop halfway down the cabin and ask an aisle seat passenger to take firm hold of the elastic strips and manoeuvre them to keep the Dakota level while he went to the toilet. Needless to say, this usually took quite a long time.

Additional revenue was earned from the participation of the Dakotas in TV programmes and movies, often repainted in temporary markings. G-AMPY was hired to make promotional appearances in period Northwest Airlines livery to commemorate the 60th anniversary of that US carrier. During these appearances the aircraft carried the US period registration NW21711 as well as its own UK registration. Painted as such, the aircraft made a memorable appearance at the Fighter Meet air show at North Weald airfield in 1986, flying in formation with a Northwest Orient Airlines Boeing 747 'Jumbo Jet'. The Dakota was still wearing the livery in early 1987 when it was used in ground shots for the movie *Testimony*, starring Ben Kingsley. The scenes depicted the arrival in the USA in 1949 of the composer Shostakovich as an emissary from the Soviet leader Stalin, and some Air Atlantique ground crew even found additional work as extras in the film. In 1991 another Dakota, G-AMRA, was painted up in the livery of the fictitious airline Empire Airways for scenes in the screen version of an Agatha Christie novel. It was carrying these markings when it paid a visit to the International Air Tattoo that July. In late 2001 G-AMYJ was

Dakota G-AMRA wearing the livery of the fictitious Empire Airways at the International Air Tattoo at RAF Fairford in 1991.

given a water-based repaint into camouflage for ground scenes in the Tom Hanks/Steven Spielberg Second World War TV series *Band of Brothers*. Two Air Atlantique engineers were detached to North Weald airfield to service the Dakota during the filming, and they too ended up in uniform as extras.

During the late 1980s a programme of day trips to air shows was operated each year in conjunction with Carrick Travel. The events covered in 1987 included:

2 May	Coventry–Jersey for Jersey Airport 50th Anniversary Air Day
14 June	Coventry–RAF, Church Fenton Open Day
20 June	Coventry–Beauvais, with coach transfers to/from Paris Air Show
5 July	Coventry–RAF Cranwell Open Day
18 and 19 July	Coventry–International Air Tattoo, Fairford
22 July	Cardiff–RAF Chivenor Open Day
23 July	Cardiff–RAF Brawdy Open Day
5 August	Bournemouth–RAF St Mawgan Open Day
15 August	Liverpool–RAF Valley Open Day
15 August	Coventry–RAF Valley Open Day

These flights were operated by Dakotas G-AMPY and G-AMSV, and the airline's association with Carrick Travel was to continue for many subsequent years.

Various one-off opportunities for charter flights with the Dakotas continued to present themselves during the 1990s. In 1991 the Tall Ships Race was centred around Aberdeen, and for two weeks in August G-AMPZ was kept busy carrying out sightseeing flights over the flotilla of sailing ships in the harbour. On 18 March 1993 the same aircraft, filled with reporters and cameramen, followed the last airworthy Avro Vulcan XH558 on its delivery flight from RAF Waddington to Bruntingthorpe airfield for storage, on what was thought to be the last ever Vulcan flight. In 1994 many activities were scheduled to mark the 50th anniversary of D-Day on 6 June. That year Britannia Travel advertised its intention of operating a series of Dakota flights to Normandy, and to gain media coverage G-AMPY operated a special flight out of Bournemouth for the press, civic dignitaries and D-Day veterans on 28 January. As in previous years a full programme of Dakota day trips to UK air shows was also offered for the 1994 season. Flights to Duxford, Biggin Hill, Bruntingthorpe, Fairford, Finningley and Cranfield were operated from Coventry, and the shows at North Weald, Wroughton, Biggin Hill and Duxford were served from Bournemouth (Hurn) Airport. Prices ranged from £40 (Coventry–Bruntingthorpe) to £99 (Coventry–Biggin Hill) and all were inclusive of air show admission.

On 2 June 1996 the Heathrow 50th anniversary fly-past brought the airport to a standstill for a short period while thirty-four examples of historic transport types, from Dakota to Concorde, flew along runway 27R. Air Atlantique's contribution to this unique occasion was substantial, including DH Rapide G-AIDL, two Dakotas, and DC-6A G-SIXC. By the mid-1990s the airline had built up a unique fleet of aircraft. In addition to the commercially operated aircraft, examples of historically significant RAF types had been acquired, and in 1995 the Air Atlantique Historic Fleet (AAHF) was set up to display the historic types at air shows and to offer pleasure flights in DH89 Dragon Rapide, Scottish Aviation Twin Pioneer and Percival Prentice aircraft. In order to comply with EU regulations the Dragon

Air Atlantique

PRESENT

A ONCE IN A LIFETIME EXPERIENCE!
FLY OVER THE TALL SHIPS IN THE LEGENDARY

DC3 DAKOTA

FROM

ABERDEEN AIRPORT

AUGUST 4th - 8th incl.

FLIGHTS LEAVE EVERY HOUR
COMMENCING 10.30 AM FINISH 8.00 PM
**ADVANCE RESERVATIONS: PHONE
0203 - 639067**
OR SIMPLY TURN UP ON THE
DAY & TIME OF YOUR CHOICE

★ FLIGHTS 30 MINS APPROX.
★ PLENTY OF FLIGHTS
★ NO NEED TO BOOK
★ BRING THE FAMILY
★ FARES: £25.00 ADULTS
        £15.00 CHILDREN
★ IT MAY NEVER HAPPEN AGAIN

THE TALL SHIPS RACES

Handbill promoting Air Atlantique's Dakota flights over the Tall Ships in Aberdeen Harbour in 1997.

PILOT'S NOTES

FOR

RAPIDE

Air Atlantique

The cover of the *Rapide Pilots Notes* booklet issued to pleasure flight pilots.

Rapide G-AIDL in its element over Draycott Reservoir, near Coventry. (Courtesy of Will Jarman)

Rapides had first to be equipped with modern FM Immune radio equipment, Mode S transponders, strobe lights and outside air temperature gauges. The first public appearance of the whole AAHF fleet took place at the 1996 Leicester Air Show. Dragon Rapide G-AIDL was regarded as the flagship of the AAHF fleet. This sturdy biplane had previously been used for pleasure flying duties from Caernarfon airfield by the resident operator Snowdon Mountain Aviation. When Air Atlantique took over the lease on the airfield in 1992 it also acquired Snowdon Mountain Aviation and its Dragon Rapide and renamed the operator as Air Caernarfon. The Rapide also gained the green, white and black livery of the Air Atlantique Group. Other founder members of the AAHF fleet included Percival Prentice G-APJB, which had been acquired in 1992 for restoration to flying condition. It made its first post-restoration flight on 14 June 1996, wearing RAF silver trainer livery and the serial VR259. It soon became a pleasure flying stalwart, and in 2010 was still the only example certified for passenger carriage. Another unique aircraft in the pleasure flying fleet, Twin Pioneer G-BCWF, was acquired in November 1993 from the defunct UK operator Flight One. It was flown into Coventry in and taken into a hangar for a respray into full Atlantic Airways livery, emerging thus in early December. On 9 December 1993, the 'Twin Pin' regained its original registration as G-APRS. Over the weekends of 8/9 January and 15/16 January 1994 it could be seen on static display as part of Luton Airport's open days. The

Percival Prentice VR259 awaits its next party of pleasure flyers at the 2003 Coventry Air Show.

aircraft made its first air show appearance at Duxford in July 1996 and was subsequently repainted into the 'raspberry ripple' livery of its one-time operator the RAF Empire Test Pilots School, which continued to use the aircraft from time to time. The Twin Pioneer joined the pleasure flying fleet in the summer of 1997. During its long career as part of the Air Atlantique Historic Flight it frequently showed off its very short take-off and landing performance at air shows and gained the unusual distinction of becoming the largest aircraft to land on Southport Beach. It acquired the nickname of 'Primrose', but in 2008 it had to be grounded as its wing attachment struts had almost reached the end of their fatigue life. A lengthy search produced a set in Australia, and these were shipped over to Coventry, but they were found to be incompatible with this particular machine and it was never to fly again. There was another type of aircraft that attracted much interest at Coventry, even though it never did become part of the AAHF. This was the Avro Shackleton AEW2. In June 1991 the RAF retired its last surviving examples, which were sold at auction. Two of them found their way to Coventry Airport. WR963 was the property of the Shackleton Preservation Trust and was cared for by Air Atlantique engineers until it was handed over to Avro Shackleton Charity Enterprise Training on 27 November 2008. Its companion aircraft WL790 was acquired by Air Atlantique in 1993 and was the subject of attempts to place it on the UK register so that it could perform at air shows. These efforts

Twin Pioneer G-APRS, another popular pleasure flying steed at the Coventry Air Show in 2003.

proved unsuccessful, and the major decision was taken to fly it across to the USA and place it on the US civil register. Once this was achieved it was hoped it could return to the UK and take part in air shows. It was ferried across the Atlantic in 1994 and was initially based with the Confederate Air Force (CAF) at Midland, Texas. Re-registered as N790WL, the Shackleton took part in displays at Midland and at Oklahoma City, flown by Air Atlantique's Paul Sabin. It was at the CAF air show at Midland in 2000 that an American commentator announced that it was about to 'simulate its wartime successes bombing Germany'. Apart from these events the Shackleton hardly flew and eventually a home was found for it at the Pima Air and Space Museum at Davis-Monthan AFB. It arrived there on 16 December 2007 after a 3-hour flight from Midland.

It was not just the Dakotas that got to appear on screen. During July 1994 the DC-6A G-SIXC was painted up in period Air France livery to represent that airline's DC-4 aircraft F-BBDG in scenes in the French movie *Une Femme Francais*, which were shot at Berlin (Templehof) Airport. In 2006 the same aircraft appeared as set dressing for airport scenes in the James Bond film *Casino Royale*, and the following year the other DC-6 G-APSA was repainted by KLM at Schipol in their period livery as PH-TGA for participation in the movie *Bride Flight*. It made its first public appearance in this 1950s-era colour scheme at

Shackleton AEW2 WL790 at Coventry in 1993, a year before its departure to the USA. (Courtesy of Eric Melrose)

DC-6A G-APSA painted up in the livery of its earlier operator, British Eagle International Airlines, at Coventry in 2011 (Courtesy of Eric Melrose)

the Portrush Air Show in September 2007. Many years before it joined the Air Atlantique Group G-APSA had been part of the fleet of British Eagle International Airlines. The date 6 November 2008 would mark the 40th anniversary of the collapse of this charismatic airline, and funds were raised to restore G-APSA to its British Eagle livery for participation in a series of commemorative events. As such, the airliner made appearances in 2008 at the Biggin Hill Air Fair, Blackbushe Airport, the London City Airport Fun Day air show, and the Farnborough Air Show, where a British Eagle staff reunion was taking place. Later in the year the DC-6A, flown by Julian Firth and Stewart Byers, re-enacted a former British Eagle scheduled service by flying into Innsbruck Airport. It went on to visit Berlin's Templehof Airport, where it spent some time acting as a memorial to the civil airline crews who lost their lives taking part in the Berlin Airlift. It then went on to Rotterdam Airport, the departure point of British Eagle's last service, before returning home to Coventry on 17 November 2008. Departure slots had been allocated at Heathrow for a visit to British Eagle's home base during November 2008, but were later withdrawn because of 'congestion'. Future plans for G-APSA included its conversion to a forty-passenger deluxe layout for high-end tours, but in the spring of 2009 'PSA' was found to be suffering from wing spar issues that would eventually bring about its grounding. In addition to its air show appearances Air Atlantique allowed the public a close-up view of its day-to-day operations through open days at Coventry Airport. For the modest sum of £30 per head a conducted tour of the

Dakota G-AMPY in RAF Transport Command livery, seen from a Shackleton during an open day at Coventry. (Courtesy of Eric Melrose)

hangars, including access to the interiors of some of the aircraft, was followed by a flight in a Dakota. In 2000 the future still looked bright for the Air Atlantique Group. A profit had been recorded every year since 1983, even in 1999 when cargo business dropped by two-thirds. The Cessna 152 G-HART had been converted to tailwheel configuration to provide experience for the airline's Dakota trainees and for any private pilots wishing to fly a 'taildragger'. A Cessna Citation jet was now being offered for executive charter and between times was used to ferry the company's pilots and groundcrew around. Although operations were now based at Coventry, Mike Collett still resided on Jersey and borrowed one of the company's Cessna 310 'twins' to commute to the office. Around 400 staff were now employed, although Mike Collett was heard to remark that he had felt more comfortable when the company was around half that size. The Air Atlantique Historic Flight had a total of nine airframes, including the Shackleton N790WL based in the USA, and had sufficient resources to mount the Air Atlantique Fifties Air Show, held at Coventry over the weekend of 12/13 August 2000. Among the many attractions in the static park the other Shackleton WR963 was open for inspection. Pleasure flights were on offer in Dakota G-AMPZ (still in RAF Transport Command livery), the Twin Pioneer and a Dragon Rapide. The flying programme included displays by Dassault Flamant F-AZFX, the rarely seen Howard 500 N500LN, the Dutch Dakota Association's Douglas DC-4 PH-DDS, the Emerald Airways HS748 G-BIUV, and Antonov AN-2 HA-MKF, plus multi-aircraft contributions from Air Atlantique's own fleet. These included formation fly-pasts made up of both DC-6As plus Convair 440 CS-TML and by two Percival Pembrokes plus an Anson and a Dove, both in Gulf

PROGRAMME of EVENTS

Saturday's Flying Display Programme

1400	Canberra
	Vampire & Venom
	EFTS Flight
	Flamant
	Nord 1101
	T.28 Fennec
	de Havilland Formation
1500	Hunter
	Lockheed L188 Electra
	Meteor F8
	AN - 2
	Convair 440
	Douglas DC - 6
	Avenger
1600	Comms Flight (Anson,Pembroke x2)
	Noratlas
	Howard 500
	Gnat
	Meteor NF11
	Jet Provost
	Yak C11
	Dakota Formation (7 DC 3s)
1720	DISPLAY ENDS

Sunday's Flying Display Programme

1335	Meteor F8
	Meteor NF11
	Convair 440
1400	Douglas DC - 6
	Gnat
	Sea Fury
	Mustang
	Howard 500
	AN - 2
	Vampire & Venom
1500	Noratlas
	Twin Pioneer
	Avenger
	Yak C11
	Comms Flight (Anson,Pembroke x2)
	Hunter
	Avro 748
1600	Douglas DC 4
	Lockheed L188 Electra
	Canberra
	EFTS Flight
	Flamant
	Nord 1101
1700	T.28 Fennec
	de Havilland Formation (Rapide, Dove,Heron)
	Dakota Formation (7 DC - 3s)
1725	DISPLAY ENDS

The flying display programme is subject to last minute changes, and the timings shown are only indicative.

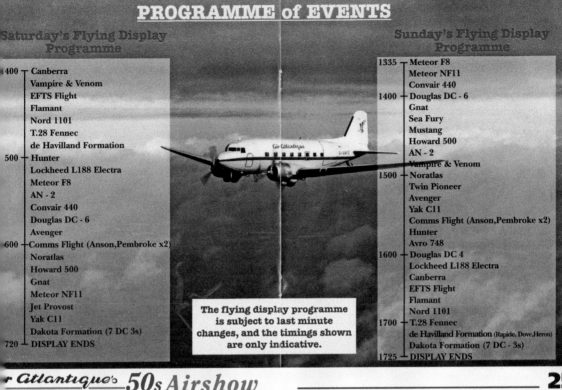

r Atlantique's 50s Airshow — 2:

The order of flying for the Air Atlantique '50s Airshow, held on 12/13 August 2000.

Aviation livery. The grand finale consisted of two fly-pasts by a formation of seven Dakotas, one of which, G-ANAF, was wearing an under-nose 'chin' radome. This highly successful display set the tone for several more 'at home' air shows in subsequent years as well as frequent appearances by the Historic Flight further afield. Anson C.21 G-VROE had been purchased by Air Atlantique in February 1998 and normally wore RAF Transport Command livery as WD413. Dove 8 G-DHDV had also been acquired in 1998 and had previously served with the Battle of Britain Memorial Flight as DH Devon VP981. Both aircraft were repainted to represent examples of the early types of aircraft operated by Gulf Air's predecessor in the 1950s and carried period 1950s UK registrations, but with the 'G' nationality prefix omitted to satisfy regulations. The Anson made several promotional outings in this livery, in June 1999 appearing at the Paris Air Show alongside Gulf Air's first Airbus A330-200, but this was just the lead up to the visit of both aircraft to the Gulf in 2000. They departed Coventry on this epic trip on 10 March 2000 and routed via Nevers, Genoa, Naples, Corfu, Santorini, Iraklion, Luxor, Jeddah and Riyadh, arriving Bahrain on 23 March. The Anson was piloted by Chris Bevan, with Richard Blech in command of the Dove. Also on the trip were engineer David Kingshott and photographer (and former airline pilot) Austin Brown. The anniversary ceremonials took place at Bahrain International Airport on 25 March, with the Anson and the Dove parked on the tarmac close to the original control tower and terminal building. On the following morning both aircraft set off to visit Qatar, Sharjah, Dubai, Abu Dhabi, Muscat, Kuwait and Saudi Arabia before returning home. The Dove was then

Meteor NF11 WM167 at the RAF Leuchars Air Show in September 2009.

Avro Anson C.21 WD413 participating in the air show at Perth, Scotland, in June 2010.

repainted back into RAF Transport Command livery as VP981, but the Anson retained its Gulf Aviation colour scheme for some time. Other flyable aircraft operated by the Historic flight at this time included:

Chipmunk G-APLO, which had been used by Air Service Training at Perth, Scotland, to train many future commercial pilots, including Mike Collett, who later acquired the aircraft. He applied an all-black livery with white training bands, RAF roundels and fin flash to represent the Chipmunk used by the Battle of Britain Memorial Flight for tailwheel training, only to have permission to fly it in these markings refused. The roundels and fin flash were then removed and the aircraft's civil registration was applied in large white lettering.

Percival Prentice G-APJB was non-airworthy when acquired by Air Atlantique in 1992 and restored to flying condition. It's first flight after restoration came on 14 June 1996. It went on to become a regular air show performer and pleasure flying mount, repainted in silver RAF trainer markings with the period serial VR259. Another Prentice, G-AOKO, was also acquired as a source of spare parts.

DH Dragon Rapide G-AKRP joined the fleet on long-term lease in 2006.

Percival Proctor 5 G-AKIU was acquired by Mike Collett in 1999 and Hornet Aviation was entrusted with its restoration to flying condition. This proved to be a lengthy process, but by 2010 this it was in the Classic Flight hangar at Coventry and was almost ready for flight.

Percival Pembroke C(PR)1 G-BXES was built for the RAF as Pembroke C.1 XL954. In 1963 it was modified to carry cameras in its fuselage for discrete photography while being flown along the air corridors into West Berlin by 60 Squadron. After acquisition and restoration by the Air Atlantique engineers it flew again on 17 February 1999, wearing its former RAF livery and serial number.

Over the weekend of 31 May/1 June 2003 Air Atlantique staged its Classic Air Show at Coventry Airport, the first event in a packed year of open days at Coventry, enthusiast's day trips to air shows and pleasure flying sessions. Throughout the two days of the air show pleasure flights were on offer using a veritable 'fleet' of Classic Flight aircraft, including the Dove, Twin Pioneer, Prentice, two Dragon Rapides and Dakota G-AMRA. Air Atlantique's contribution to the flying display included a formation of three Dakotas (G-AMPY, G-AMSV and G-ANAF), a pair of Pembrokes, and low fly-pasts and 'live' water-spraying runs by DC-6A G-APSA and Electra G-LOFE. Air Atlantique had also able to secure flying displays by many unusual visitors, including Nord Noratlas F-AVZM, Grumman Albatross 141262, Douglas DC-2 PH-AJI, and the Red Bull-schemed Sea Vixen G-CVIX, plus several early jet fighters. The static park also included many rarities such as Antonov AN-2 D-FKMA, Air Atlantique's grounded Convair 440 G-CONV, and Lockheed Electra N2RK, still under conversion to Air Atlantique's two-crew cockpit layout. Engine run-ups by Shackleton WR963 added to the air of nostalgia, and the weekend was only marred by the tragic loss of the *Spirit of St Louis* replica and its pilot on the Saturday. During the heyday of the air show

Dakota G-AMRA performs a steep turn during the Sywell Air Show in August 2010.

The classic nose/engine profile of the Dakota. G-AMRA seen at the Sywell Air Show in August 2010.

Rapide G-AGTM *Sybille* at the Sywell Air Show in August 2010.

Rapide TX310 on pleasure flying duties at the Perth Air Show in June 2010.

Anson C.21 WD413 is dwarfed by an RAF C-17 Globemaster at the RAF Leuchars Air Show in September 2001.

Percival Pembroke XL954 during its display at the Coventry Air Show in 2003.

De Havilland Dove G-DHDV still in partial Gulf Aviation livery at the 2003 Coventry Air Show.

Dakota G-AMRA on pleasure flying duties at the 2003 Coventry Air Show.

Pleasure flying Rapide G-AIDL at the Coventry Air Show in 2003.

Dakota G-AMSV with Pollution Control titles at the 2003 Coventry Air Show.

Dakota G-AMPY flying at the 2003 Coventry Air Show.

A classic nose/engine view of DC-6A G-APSA at the Coventry Air Show in 2003.

DC-6A G-APSA taxies out for its display at the 2003 Coventry Air Show.

DC-6A G-APSA sprays the runway (and the front rows of the crowd) with water during its display at the 2003 Coventry Air Show.

DC-6A SIXC taxies in at the conclusion of its display at Coventry in 2003.

Electra G-LOFE strains against its wheel brakes before taking off to display at the 2003 Coventry Air Show.

A low and slow fly-past by Electra G-LOFE at the 2003 Coventry Air Show.

Electra G-LOFE demonstrates its spraying gear during the 2003 Coventry Air Show.

years Air Atlantique placed an advertisement in the aviation press seeking additional pilots to assist with pleasure flying. Only pilots with considerable tailwheel experience would be considered. Renumeration was to be on an expenses-only basis, but plenty of flying was promised, along with conversion training onto unusual aircraft types.

4

The Rundown

The year 2003 might well be regarded as the high point for the Air Atlantique Group, as from that time the organisation began experiencing problems that were to lead to its eventual breakup. For some time the management had been trying to get its proposals for a new terminal building at Coventry approved, but in December that year Warwickshire District Council announced that these would not now be considered until the end of 2004. Before this could take place, however, in February 2004 the TUI holiday organisation reached a deal to take over the lease and operation of the airport from Air Atlantique. TUI announced plans to use Coventry as a base for low-cost flights by its airline Thomsonfly, with Boeing 737 services commencing on 31 March 2004 from a temporary terminal building. The council was said to have lost confidence in Air Atlantique, who it accused of 'developing the airport by stealth'. Approval had been given for the construction of a safety area at each end of the runway, and while this was taking place Air Atlantique had also added an aircraft turning circle at the Bagington end of the runway and carried out other building work without approval. The activities of the historic aircraft fleet continued to attract visitors, and on 17 December 2005 Dakota G-AMRA was used to operate a day of pleasure flights from Coventry to commemorate the 70th anniversary of the maiden flight of this much-loved aircraft type. Although part of the Classic Flight, this aircraft was still available as a backup for cargo flights if needed, and during the winter of 2005/6 was used for a freight run to the Channel Islands. The year 2006 saw a brief return to scheduled passenger services when Atlantic Air Transport, trading as Atlantic Express, began operating Jersey–Stansted schedules on 27 May. Two ATR-42 turbo-prop aircraft maintained a twice-daily service throughout the summer, and the airline announced that for the summer of 2007 the frequency would be increased to three round trips each day; however, the management then thought again, and these services were terminated at the end of 2006. In December 2006 Mike Collett announced that he had plans for a huge expansion of the historic aircraft side of the business; although, now that Thomsonfly was playing such a dominant role at Coventry he was looking at an alternative location for the historic airframes. In the end this proved unnecessary as on 9 November 2008 Thomsonfly ceased its operations out of Coventry, having seen its own application for a new terminal rejected. On 16 December 2007 Air Atlantique staged a celebration at Coventry to mark the

ATR-42 G-DRFC wearing Atlantic Express titles at Jersey in August 2008. (Courtesy of Rosemary Ames)

seventy-second birthday of the Dakota, with pleasure flights being operated by G-AMRA, wearing Classic Flight titles and named *Rudolph* for the occasion. On 12 February 2008 Mike Collett held a press conference at Coventry to announce his latest project. For the coming summer he was considering the operation of scheduled passenger flights between Coventry and the Imperial War Museum airfield at Duxford. The flights would take place over each weekend and would initially use the Percival Prentice. If demand for seats proved sufficiently encouraging he would consider substituting larger Dragon Rapide or Dove aircraft. However, his optimistic plans would soon be dashed by an announcement from Europe.

For a number of years Air Atlantique's passenger-configured Dakotas G-AMPY and G-AMRA had been operating under Civil Aviation Authority exemptions, which allowed them to avoid the much stricter safety regulations introduced on air transport carriers throughout the EU. These rules required passenger aircraft to be fitted with public-address systems, weather radar, cockpit voice recorders, bullet-proof doors separating the flight deck from the passenger cabin, emergency cabin lighting and oxygen, and passenger evacuation slides among many other items. Air Atlantique pointed out that they were operating under special exemptions granted by the Civil Aviation Authority (CAA) in recognition of the unique nature of their operations. Their Dakotas never flew above 5,000 ft on pleasure flights, and when they were on the ground the sill of the passenger cabin door was only 4 ft above the ground, making evacuation slides unnecessary and impossible to install.

However, this situation was to end on 16 July 2008 when the European Aviation Safety Agency was to take over from the CAA as the designated UK airworthiness authority. From then onwards, if Air Atlantique wanted to continue carrying passengers in the Dakotas all of the very expensive modifications would first have to be carried out. Compared to modern airliners the Dakotas had very low utilisation and produced little revenue, and to implement the requirements would simply not be cost-effective. Unless some way around the rules could be found, passenger operations by the Dakotas would cease at midnight on 15 July 2008. A programme of special events was announced to offer as many people as possible their last chance to fly in a Dakota in the UK. A farewell tour of Britain would be carried out by the two passenger-configured Dakotas between mid-April and mid-July, with pleasure flying at each stop and culminating in a day of local flights at Coventry on 15 July. On that date, G-AMPY carried out Air Atlantique's final fare-paying Dakota passenger flight. This aircraft was still flown on special occasions, and, still wearing RAF Transport Command livery as KK116, it visited Berlin (Templehof) Airport that year as part of the

Dakota G-AMPY, alias 'KK116', at Edinburgh during its 'Farewell to the Dakota' UK pleasure flying tour in 2008. (Courtesy of Jeff Henderson)

commemorations of the 60th anniversary of the Berlin Airlift. By then many of the other Dakotas had been retired and were serving as sources of spares at Coventry, although G-AMPY and G-ANAF were still on lease to the RVL Group for marine surveillance on behalf of the Maritime and Coastguard Agency and remained airworthy and operational at Coventry. Some of their sister ships had been found good homes elsewhere. G-AMHJ had been donated to the Assault Glider Trust in November 2002 after two years in storage, and G-AMYJ went to the Yorkshire Air Museum at Elvington in December 2001. The unfortunate Convair 440 G-CONV was never restored to flying condition. In 2007 it was transported by road to the Carluke Garden Centre in Lanarkshire, where plans had been announced to convert it to into deluxe bed-and-breakfast accommodation. These plans were later changed, however, and the airframe was instead converted into a beauty salon in the garden centre grounds.

Back at Coventry, tragedy struck on 17 August 2008 when former Air Atlantique pilot and now Chief Training Captain of RVL, Sybille Gautrey, was among those lost when her

The rather spartan interior of Dakota G-AMPY during its 2008 farewell pleasure flying tour of the UK. (Courtesy of Jeff Henderson)

Cessna 402 G-EYES collided with a light aircraft while both machines were inbound to the airport.

In October 2008 Atlantic Airlines announced that it would be merging with West Air Sweden to form West Atlantic Airlines, with its corporate headquarters in Sweden. For the time being, however, both airlines continued to operate independently.

Although the Dakota passenger flights had come to an end and the cargo operations were no longer part of the Air Atlantique Group, Mike Collett's prized collection of historic aircraft continued to thrive under the Classic Flight banner, with Steve Bridgewater as its Commercial Manager and an initial 'fleet' of eighteen propeller-driven aircraft and nine vintage jets. The Classic Flight also announced plans to sell shares in its aircraft for £2,000–£3,000 each. Shareholders would be entitled to free flights as passengers in the aircraft wherever this was permitted. At the end of 2008 the Classic Flight Club was launched to offer enthusiasts a closer connection with the Classic Flight aircraft. Two levels

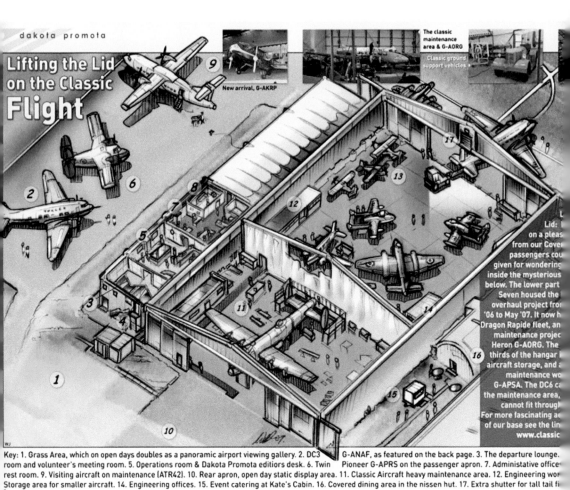

Key: 1. Grass Area, which on open days doubles as a panoramic airport viewing gallery. 2. DC3 G-ANAF, as featured on the back page. 3. The departure lounge. room and volunteer's meeting room. 5. Operations room & Dakota Promota editiors desk. 6. Twin Pioneer G-APRS on the passenger apron. 7. Administative office rest room. 9. Visiting aircraft on maintenance (ATR42). 10. Rear apron, open day static display area. 11. Classic Aircraft heavy maintenance area. 12. Engineering wor Storage area for smaller aircraft. 14. Engineering offices. 15. Event catering at Kate's Cabin. 16. Covered dining area in the nissen hut. 17. Extra shutter for tall tail fi

A 2007 artist's cutaway diagram of the proposed interior layout of Hangar 7 at Coventry. (Courtesy of Will Jarman)

of membership were offered. Standard Membership cost £65 per annum and included four vouchers for 50 per cent off the price of a pleasure flight. For those able to contribute more than £500 per annum, Gold Membership came with an unlimited supply of half-price pleasure flights. Gold Members would also be eligible to join the Classic Jet Support Team and register for a chance to fly in one of the two-seater jets on transit flights to air shows and on certain other occasions. Both categories of members would receive the quarterly club magazine *The Meteor*, invitations to members-only events, and entry to a dedicated club marquee at air shows. In December 2008 the Classic Flight held a night photo shoot, at which several of its aircraft ran up their engines under floodlights. Originally there were plans for the Classic Flight Club to be developed in association with Kemble-based Delta Jets and to transfer the Coventry resident aircraft to Kemble. A visitor centre was to be built at Kemble, along with two new hangars to house all but the largest exhibits. In the end the projected move to Kemble did not take place. Instead, Hangar 7 at Coventry was converted into AIRBASE, the new home of the Air Atlantique Classic Flight. In addition to the thirty or so classic aircraft on show, visitors were offered taxi rides around the airfield in a DC-6A and could even experience aerobatic manoeuvres in a Chipmunk. Classic Flight Club members were entitled to free admission to AIRBASE.

At the end of 2009 a near-disastrous development had to be overcome. On 8 December Coventry Airport was suddenly forced to close down due to 'financial reasons' and it was revealed that West Midlands International Airport Ltd, which owned the airport, was due to appear in the High Court to respond to a winding-up petition. All the Air Atlantique Group's operations were temporarily transferred to Birmingham Airport, but following the buyout of the Coventry Airport by Sir Peter Rigby's Patriot Group in April 2010 the airport was able to reopen and new offices were set up on the south side. By then, however, the Atlantic Airlines Operational and Line Maintenance Centre had been relocated to East Midlands Airport and the cargo services had been transferred across. Although Coventry Airport was still officially closed on 13 December 2009 this did not deter the Classic Flight from staging another night photo shoot on that date. This time the aircraft on view 'under the lights' included DH Heron G-AORG in Jersey Airlines markings, Dakota G-ANAF (now in a new red and black livery), a DH Venom, Meteor NF11 and Avro Anson. On 11 May 2010 a major new attraction was added to the collection. HS Nimrod MR2 XV232 arrived in the skies over Coventry from RAF Kinloss and performed two fly-pasts before landing. Destined for the AIRBASE museum, its maintenance documents were then handed over to Mike Collett. On 15 February 2012 the Classic Aircraft Trust was officially launched as a charity-based arm of the Classic Flight, with Tim Skeet as its Chairman. Mike Collett donated all his airframes held at AIRBASE to the trust to ensure they continued to receive the financial support and expert care needed to keep them flying. The flyable aircraft were to be maintained and operated by Air Atlantique under a formal service agreement. He was quoted as saying:

The costs of keeping twenty-odd aircraft flying are pretty frightening. When we were busy with cargo and passenger operations and had a reasonably large annual income it was possible to pay for things like annual checks and engine changes. We haven't got the active business we used to have. We could have put the aircraft up for sale to individual buyers to look after them, but there was always the chance they could go

Nimrod MR2 XV232 taxies in at AIRBASE after its delivery flight to Coventry on 11 May 2010.

abroad. The alternative was to establish the Trust. With the charity we will be able to have a fund-raising operation to pay for the cost of making the aircraft fly again.

This encouraging development was, however, followed by the shock announcement in September 2012 that AIRBASE at Coventry was to close at the end of that month. The collection of aircraft there was to be relocated to Newquay Airport, with a deadline for vacating the Coventry premises of 31 July 2013. A spokesman for AIRBASE said that 'the writing was on the wall' once the airport's new owner Sir Peter Rigby announced plans for a technology and distribution park to be known as the Coventry Gateway Scheme on green belt land around the airport. This would create around 10,000 jobs, but AIRBASE was in its way and had to go. Classic Aircraft Trust Chairman Tim Skeet said, 'There isn't the footfall at Coventry. Visitor numbers were never particularly impressive. We have to look at ways of sustaining sources of revenue from the tourist industry.' Among the reasons given for choosing Newquay Airport were that it was within the Cornwall Aerohub Enterprise Zone and so the rent would be considerably less, with no rates payable for the first year of occupancy. The first AIRBASE aircraft to be flown to Newquay was the Auster Autocrat G-JAYI, on 5 January 2013. The rest of the collection followed at intervals, but Shackleton WR963 had to remain at Coventry as the cost of road transport was unacceptably high.

On 31 March 2013 the Classic Air Force reopened to the public at Newquay Airport. Its new home was Hangar 404, which had previously housed three RAF Nimrod maritime patrol aircraft and, at 63,000 sq ft, was the largest building in Cornwall. Admission to the

The AIRBASE hangar at Coventry. Gracing the tarmac outside are two Canberras, a Venom, and Nimrod MR2 XV232.

grand opening event was free, and 2,554 visitors visited that day. The opening ceremony included a brief flying display by Jet Provost T3A XM424, and pleasure flights in Dragon Rapide G-AGTM were on offer. Once the museum was up and running two new exhibits were donated – BAC One-Eleven ZH763 and Vickers VC-10 ZA148. By 20 April that year around 12,000 visitors had passed through the turnstiles and around 100 of them had been carried aloft on pleasure flights. One aircraft that was not destined to join the museum at Newquay was Dakota G-AMRA, which had been acquired by Air Service Berlin for sightseeing flights, and flew out of Coventry on 30 July 2013 on delivery. All seemed to be progressing well at the new Newquay site, but in early March 2015 the landlords announced that the museum was going to be relocated to a new landside location at the airport. In response the Classic Air Force then announced that the Newquay museum would close at the end of the month, as the proposed new location was unsuitable and would render the operation financially unviable. The smaller flyable exhibits would be flown back to Coventry, where all operations would now be concentrated around the former Hangar 7, now to be developed as AIRBASE. However, larger aircraft such as the VC-10 would be too costly to relocate and would have to stay at Newquay. A statement published on the Classic Air Force Facebook site said, 'This has been an incredibly hard decision, but the costs of maintaining two attractions are too much to justify, given our status as a charity. Our focus now is on our traditional home here in Coventry, where we'll be doing more flying, more events, and adding more to see and do than ever before.' Since

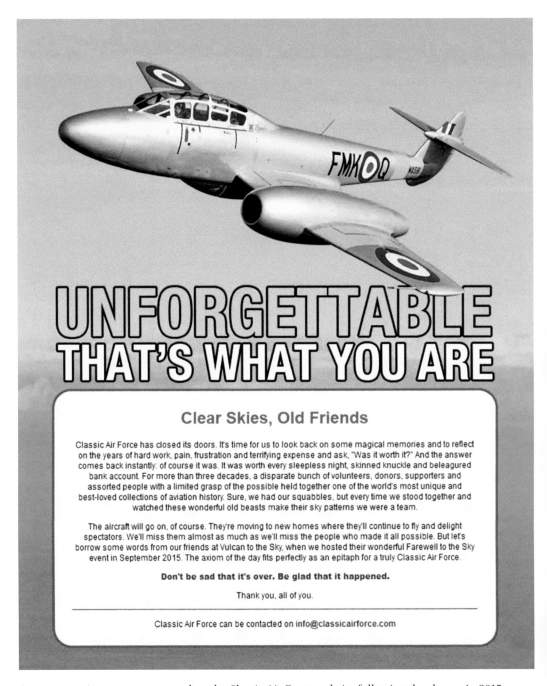

UNFORGETTABLE
THAT'S WHAT YOU ARE

Clear Skies, Old Friends

Classic Air Force has closed its doors. It's time for us to look back on some magical memories and to reflect on the years of hard work, pain, frustration and terrifying expense and ask, "Was it worth it?" And the answer comes back instantly: of course it was. It was worth every sleepless night, skinned knuckle and beleagured bank account. For more than three decades, a disparate bunch of volunteers, donors, supporters and assorted people with a limited grasp of the possible held together one of the world's most unique and best-loved collections of aviation history. Sure, we had our squabbles, but every time we stood together and watched these wonderful old beasts make their sky patterns we were a team.

The aircraft will go on, of course. They're moving to new homes where they'll continue to fly and delight spectators. We'll miss them almost as much as we'll miss the people who made it all possible. But let's borrow some words from our friends at Vulcan to the Sky, when we hosted their wonderful Farewell to the Sky event in September 2015. The axiom of the day fits perfectly as an epitaph for a truly Classic Air Force.

Don't be sad that it's over. Be glad that it happened.

Thank you, all of you.

Classic Air Force can be contacted on info@classicairforce.com

A message to its supporters posted on the Classic Air Force website following the closure in 2015.

the move to Newquay the museum site at Coventry had only been open at weekends for limited viewing, but now a new reception area, shop and café would be created there, and additional attractions such as flight simulators would be installed. There were plans to celebrate the return to Coventry with a low-key air show, and on 2 May 2015 this duly took place, under the name 'AIRBASE Gets Airborne'. Low-key it may have been, but it was well-attended, and its success led to the announcement of a Bagington Air Pageant, to take place that July. This included a recreation of a 1940s-style air race with entrants including an Auster Autocrat, Chipmunk, Proctor and Gemini, and a display by a Spitfire PR XIX. It looked like Air Atlantique was set for a new beginning at Coventry as the custodian and operator of a sizeable fleet of classic aircraft and perhaps as the organiser of 1950s-style air shows as well, but in August 2015 Mike Collett, now seventy-two years old, announced his impending retirement. His various remaining businesses were to be offered for disposal by management buyouts to allow him to concentrate on his first love – the restoration of vintage aircraft to flying condition. AIRBASE was to be closed down in October 2015 and the Classic Air Force aircraft were to be disposed of by early 2016. Of the thirty-six airframes in the collection, five were to be auctioned off by Bonhams at Goodwood. These

Don't be sad that it's over. Be glad that it happened.

comprised Anson WD413, Chipmunk G-APLO, Dragon Rapide TX310, Vampire T55 XJ771 and Proctor 5 G-AKIU. Bonhams estimated that the five aircraft should fetch a total of more than £5,000 at auction. The rest of the aircraft were to be sold privately, with the proviso that the new owners should keep the aircraft in flying condition. In his announcement Mike Collett said:

The absolute essential is that they keep flying. These are living pieces of history, capable of teaching piloting and engineering skills that could otherwise be lost. Our commitment has always been to keep these aircraft alive and operational, rather than let them become dead museum pieces. All other considerations being second to that, I'm open to suggestions. If a committed, well-funded organisation puts a convincing proposition to me then it may well be possible for the whole collection to pass into new ownership. In many ways that's my favourite scenario ... I'm not looking for a quick result. I'm committed to finding the right owners or partners. I'm quite happy if it takes a year to find the right homes for the remainder. Once I'm sure that these unique aeroplanes will keep on flying for future generations then I'll feel I've done my job.

Appendix 1

Fleet Survivors

In 2019 examples of the former Air Atlantique Group fleet could still be found scattered throughout the world, some as museum pieces and some fulfilling quite unusual new roles. These are some of the airframes still to be found in the UK.

- Dakota G-AMYJ was donated by Air Atlantique to the Yorkshire Air Museum at Elvington. Repainted in RAF camouflage, it was still present there in March 2019.

- After retirement by Air Atlantique in June 2000, Dakota G-AMHJ was stored at Coventry before being donated to the Assault Glider Trust in November 2002. In November 2015 it was presented to the Metherington Airfield Visitor Centre. It was still there in wartime RAF markings in March 2019.

- Repainted in RAF markings as FZ625, Dakota G-AMPO was relocated to RAF Lyneham and dedicated as a memorial to the Air Despatch Group in June 2002. By 2019 it was on display outside RAF Brize Norton.

- In May 2016 Canberra B2 WK163 was taken over by the Vulcan to the Sky trust and transported to Robin Hood Airport, Doncaster, for eventual restoration to air show condition.

- After retirement by Atlantic Airlines the DC-6A freighter G-SIXC was moved to the perimeter of Coventry Airport and converted into the DC-6 Diner. This closed to the public on 28 September 2017, but in March 2019 the airframe was still located there awaiting an uncertain future. Also in March 2019, the airline's other DC-6A G-APSA was still resident at Coventry Airport in British Eagle International Airlines livery. Both DC-6As were acquired by the South Wales Aircraft Museum in 2020, and will be moved from Coventry to St Athan for preservation.

- In July 2018 the Twin Pioneer G-APRS was purchased by farmer Martyn Steedman for conversion into 'glamping' holiday accommodation in Scotland. With wings removed it was taken by road to Mains Farm, Thornhill, near Stirling for reassembly. It was scheduled to reopen for its new function during the summer of 2019, next to the *Sea King* helicopter already in use for the same purpose on the site.

- Convair 440 G-CONV was purchased in 2007 by the Carluke Garden Centre in Lanarkshire and was transported there by road. It was originally earmarked for conversion into deluxe bed-and-breakfast accommodation in the grounds there, but this plan was not proceeded with. Instead, it was gifted to the owner's daughter for conversion into a hair and beauty salon, opening as the Runway Studios in September 2017.

- In June 2019 DH Dove G-DHDV was present at Duxford in RAF livery as VP981.

- Shackleton AEW2 WR963 was still present at Coventry Airport during 2019. It is well preserved and its Griffon engines are run up regularly.

- During the summer of 2019 the former 'spares ship' Anson TX226 was under restoration at the Montrose Heritage Air Station in Scotland.

- After the closure of AIRBASE the museum at Newquay Airport reopened under new ownership as the Cornwall Aviation Heritage Centre. Among the many airframes and cockpits exhibited there in 2019 was Canberra T4 WJ874.

- In 2019 DH Sea Devon C.20 G-SDEV/XK895 moved from Newquay to a new home at the South Wales Aircraft Museum at St Athan, Glamorgan.

- Dakota G-ANAF was being operated in RAF markings as KP220 by Aero Legends in 2020.

- Twin Pioneer G-AZHJ was acquired by the South Wales Aircraft Museum in summer 2020 and moved to St Athan for preservation.

- By early 2021 Proctor 5 G-AKIU had been completely restored to flying condition and was being advertised for sale at £110,000.

- Vampire T.11 WZ507 was airworthy at Coventry in summer 2020.

- Anson T.21 G-VROE/WD413 was active at Sleap in 2019.

- Pembroke C.1 G-BNPU/XL929 had been acquired by the South Wales Aircraft Museum and moved to St Athan for preservation in summer 2020.

Appendix 2

Aircraft used/displayed by the Air Atlantique Group during its lifetime. (NB: some airframes were acquired for spares use only.)

Douglas C-47 Dakotas: G-AMCA, G-AMHJ, G-AMPO, G-AMPY, G-AMPZ, G-AMRA, G-AMSV, G-AMYJ, G-ANAF, G-APML, G-DAKK

Douglas DC-6A/DC-6B: G-APSA, G-SIXA, G-SIXB, G-SIXC

British Aerospace ATP: G-BTPA, G-BTPC, G-BTPE, G-BTPF, G-BTPG, G-BTPH, G-BTP,J G-BTPL, G-BTTO, G-BUUP, G-BUUR, G-MANC, G-MANH, G-MANM, G-MANO, G-OOAF, G-OBWP

Lockheed L-188 Electra: G-FIJR, G-FIJV, G-FIZU, G-LOFA, G-LOFB, G-LOFC, G-LOFD, G-LOFE, N360Q, LN-FOI/L/N/O (stored on behalf of Fred Olsen AirTransport pending disposal)

Boeing 737 srs 300F: G-JMCL, G-JMCM, G-JMCO, G-JMCP, G-JMCT, G-JMCU

Boeing 737 srs 400F: G-JMCB, G-JMCH, G-JMCJ, G-JMCK, G-JMCR, G-JMCS, G-JMCV, G-JMCX

Antonov AN-72–100: ES-NOI

ATR-42: G-IONA, G-RHUM

Auster J/1 Autocrat: G-JAYI

Beech B55 Baron: G-RICK

Bristol 170: G-BISU

Britten-Norman Trislander: G-AZLJ

Cessna 152: G-BPBG, G-HART (tailwheel conversion)

Cessna 310: G-BBBX, G-BODY, G-SOUL

Cessna 402: G-EYES, G-NOSE

Cessna 404: G-MIND, G-EXEX, G-TASK, G-LEAF

Cessna 406: G-FIND, G-TURF, G-TWIG, EI-CKY

Cessna Citation 1: G-LOFT

Cessna Citation II: N22GA

Convair 440: CS-TML (later G-CONV)

De Havilland DH89A Dragon Rapide: G-AKRP, G-AGTM, G-AIDL

De Havilland Dove/Devon: G-DHDV (Dove 8), G-APSO (Dove 5), G-ARHW (Dove 8), G-BWWC (Devon), G-BWFB (Devon), G-SDEV (Sea Devon)

Lockheed L-100 Hercules: ZS-JIV

Maule MX7-180A: G-LOFM

Percival P.40 Prentice: G-APJB, G-AOKO

Percival Proctor 5: G-AKIU

Piper PA-28 Warrior II: G-BRFM

Piper PA-39 Twin Commanche: G-AVKL

Piper PA-31 Navajo ChieftainL: EI-CEC

Scottish Aviation Twin Pioneer: G-APRS, G-AZHJ

Scottish Aviation Jetstream 31: G-JURA

Shorts 360: EI-CMG (later N360AR)

Swearingen SA227AC Metro: G-BUKA

Avro Anson: G-VROE, TX226, TX235, OO-CFA

Avro Shackleton AEW2: WL790 (later N790WL), WR963

De Havilland (Canada) Chipmunk: G-APLO

De Havilland Vampire T.55: G-HELV

De Havilland Venom: G-DHVM, G-VENM

English Electric Canberra B.2/6: G-BVWC

English Electric Canberra T.4: G-CDSX

Gloster Meteor NF.11: G-LOSM

Gloster Meteor T.7: G-BWMF

Hunting Percival Jet Provost T.3A: G-BWDS

Hunting Percival Jet Provost T.5A: G-JPRO

Hunting Percival P.66 Pembroke: G-BXES, G-BNPU

Appendix 3

Dakota and DC-6A freight flights during the winter of 1993/4.

Dakota Movements

18 November	G-AMPZ. Early morning service Manchester-Dublin. Evening charter flight for Ford Motor Company Coventry–Saarbrucken (Germany).
19 November	G-AMPZ. Ford charter Coventry–Saarbrucken.
	G-AMRA. Coventry-Belfast service.
24 November	G-AMPZ. Parcelforce service Coventry–Edinburgh.
7 and 8 December	G-AMRA and G-AMPZ. Night mail services Leeds/Bradford–Bristol.
8 December	G-AMRA. Parcelforce service Coventry–Edinburgh.
9 December	G-AMRA. Afternoon cargo services Cardiff–Maastricht–Liverpool and positioning flight to Coventry.
17 December	G-AMRA. Coventry–Brussels. Evening service Coventry–Gothenburg.
	G-AMPZ. Mail service Bristol–Stansted.
22 and 23 December	G-AMRA. Coventry–Brussels (supplement to DC-6 service).
27 December	G-AMPZ. Night service Leeds/Bradford–Gothenburg.
18 January	G-AMPZ. Luton–Lelystad (Netherlands).
21 January early hours.	G-AMPZ. East Midlands–Liverpool–Norwich mail service in
22 January	G-AMPZ. Early evening service Stansted–Newcastle.
28 January	G-AMRA. Daytime freight service Coventry–Belfast.

DC-6A Services

19 November	G-SIXC. Rotterdam–Sumburgh (Shetland) oil-related charter.
24 November	G-APSA. Coventry–Cologne–Luton freight service. Positioning flight back to Coventry.

24 and 25 November	G-SIXC. Evening services Coventry–Cologne (replacing Channel Express Electra).
9 December	G-APSA. Flight as per 24/25 November.
	G-SIXC. Freight service East Midlands–Frankfurt for Lufthansa, in place of Boeing 737.
23 December	G-APSA. Edinburgh–Amsterdam flight.
24 December	G-SIXC. Pamplona (Spain)–Coventry service.

During the above period both DC-6As were also frequently chartered by Hunting Cargo Airlines when their own Lockheed Electras were not available. From 3 January to 4 February Air Atlantique operated Luton–Brussels flights under contract to DHL, using one or the other of the two DC-6As.

Acknowledgements

Throughout the preparation of this book I have been helped by many people and organisations who have allowed me to use their images as illustrations, supplied me with anecdotes and data, and encouraged me along the way. The author would like to thank the following people/organisations for permission to use copyright material in this book and for their help in other ways: David Jefferey, Linton Chilcott, Will Jarman, Glen Fricker, Rosemary Amy, Tony Perry, Geoff Hill, Eric Melrose, Michael Little, Paul Sabin, Simon Brooke, Jeff Henderson, Robert O'Brien, Frooi Poulsen, Alexander Rankin, David Depledge, Robert Smith, Mike Heap, Raymond Oostergo, Mike Collett, Connor Stait at Amberley Publishing, Gordon Smith at Key Publishing, members of the Air-Britain AB-IX and Scotavnet aviation forums, and especially my wife Hazel. Reference was made to material in many publications, including the *Atlantique Antics* newsletter, the FlightGlobal Archive, *Propliner* magazine, *Air-Britain Aviation World* magazine, and the marvellous book *Aircraft of the Classic Flight* by Steve Bridgewater (Classic Flight Productions, 2010).

Every attempt has been made to seek permission for copyright material used in this book; however, if I have inadvertently used copyright material without mission/ acknowledgement I apologise and will make the necessary correction at the first opportunity.

The smallest member of the Air Atlantique fleet. Auster J/1 Autocrat in the hangar at Coventry during one of the open days. (courtesy of Eric Melrose)

DC-6A in British Eagle livery at the SBAC Farnborough Air Show in July 2008. (courtesy of Eric Melrose)